The Quintessence of Ibsenism

NOW COMPLETED TO THE DEATH OF IBSEN

BERNARD SHAW

The Quintessence of Ibsenism

NOW COMPLETED TO THE DEATH OF IBSEN

A DRAMABOOK

 HILL AND WANG · NEW YORK

A division of Farrar, Straus and Giroux

Copyright, 1913, by George Bernard Shaw
Standard Book Number: 8090–0509–3
Library of Congress Catalog Card Number: 57–7899

Published by Hill and Wang, Inc. by special arrangement
with the Public Trustee, London, England, and
The Society of Authors, London, England.

FIRST DRAMABOOK EDITION AUGUST 1957

15 16 17 18

Manufactured in the United States of America
by The Colonial Press Inc.

CONTENTS

PREFACE TO THE THIRD EDITION

SINCE the last edition of this book was printed, war, pestilence and famine have wrecked civilization and killed a number of people of whom the first batch is calculated as not less than fifteen millions. Had the gospel of Ibsen been understood and heeded, these fifteen millions might have been alive now; for the war was a war of ideals. Liberal ideals, Feudal ideals, National ideals, Dynastic ideals, Republican ideals, Church ideals, State ideals, and Class ideals, bourgeois and proletarian, all heaped up into a gigantic pile of spiritual high explosive, and then shovelled daily into every house with the morning milk by the newspapers, needed only a bomb thrown at Serajevo by a handful of regicide idealists to blow the centre out of Europe. Men with empty phrases in their mouths and foolish fables in their heads have seen each other, not as fellow-creatures, but as dragons and devils, and have slaughtered each other accordingly. Now that our frenzies are forgotten, our commissariats disbanded, and the soldiers they fed demobilized to starve when they cannot get employment in mending what we broke, even the iron-mouthed Ibsen, were he still alive, would perhaps spare us, disillusioned wretches as we are, the well-deserved "I told you so."

Not that there is any sign of the lesson being taken to heart. Our reactions from Militarist idealism into

Pacifist idealism will not put an end to war: they are only a practical form of the *reculer pour mieux sauter*. We still cannot bring ourselves to criticize our ideals, because that would be a form of self-criticism. The vital force that drives men to throw away their lives and those of others in the pursuit of an imaginative impulse, reckless of its apparent effect on human welfare, is, like all natural forces, given to us in enormous excess to provide against an enormous waste. Therefore men, instead of economizing it by consecrating it to the service of their highest impulses, grasp at a phrase in a newspaper article, or in the speech of a politician on a vote-catching expedition, as an excuse for exercising it violently, just as a horse turned out to grass will gallop and kick merely to let off steam. The shallowness of the ideals of men ignorant of history is their destruction.

But I cannot spend the rest of my life drawing the moral of the war. It must suffice to say here that as war throws back civilization inevitably, leaving everything worse than it was, from razors and scissors to the characters of the men that make and sell and buy them, old abuses revive eagerly in a world that dreamed it had got rid of them for ever; old books on morals become new and topical again; and old prophets stir in their graves and are read with a new sense of the importance of their message. That is perhaps why a new edition of this book is demanded.

In spite of the temptation to illustrate it afresh by the moral collapse of the last ten years, I have left the book untouched. To change a pre-war book into a post-war book would in this case mean interpreting Ibsen in the light of a catastrophe of which he was unaware. Nobody can pretend to say what view he would have taken of it. He might have thought the demolition of three monstrous idealist empires cheap at the cost of fifteen million idealists' lives. Or he might have seen in the bourgeois republics which have superseded them a more deeply entrenched fortification of idealism at its suburban worst. So I have refrained from tampering with what I wrote when I, too, was as pre-war as Ibsen.

G. B. S.

1922.

PREFACE: 1913

In the pages which follow I have made no attempt to tamper with the work of the bygone man of thirty-five who wrote them. I have never admitted the right of an elderly author to alter the work of a young author, even when the young author happens to be his former self. In the case of a work which is a mere exhibition of skill in conventional art, there may be some excuse for the delusion that the longer the artist works on it the nearer he will bring it to perfection. Yet even the victims of this delusion must see that there is an age limit to the process, and that though a man of forty-five may improve the workmanship of a man of thirty-five, it does not follow that a man of fifty-five can do the same.

When we come to creative art, to the living word of a man delivering a message to his own time, it is clear that any attempt to alter this later on is simply fraud and forgery. As I read the old Quintessence of Ibsenism I may find things that I see now at a different angle, or correlate with so many things then unnoted by me that they take on a different aspect. But though this may be a reason for writing another book, it is not a reason for altering an existing one. What I have written I have written, said Pilate, thinking (rightly, as it turned out) that his blunder might prove truer than its revision by the elders; and what he said after a lapse of twenty-one seconds I may very well say after a lapse of twenty-one years.

However, I should not hesitate to criticize my earlier work if I thought it likely to do any mischief that criticism can avert. But on reading it through I have no doubt that it is as much needed in its old form as ever it was. Now that Ibsen is no longer frantically abused, and is safe in the Pantheon, his message is in worse danger of being forgotten or ignored than when he was in the pillory. Nobody now dreams of calling me a "muck ferreting dog" because I think Ibsen a great teacher. I will not go so far as to say I wish they did; but I do say that the most effective way of shutting our minds against a great man's ideas is to take them for granted and admit he was great and have done with him. It really matters very little whether Ibsen was a great man or not: what does matter is his message and the need of it.

That people are still interested in the message is proved by the history of this book. It has long been out of print in England; but it has never been out of demand. In spite of the smuggling of unauthorized American editions, which I have winked at because the absence of an English reprint was my own fault (if it be a fault not to be able to do more than a dozen things at a time), the average price of copies of the original edition stood at twenty-four shillings some years ago, and is no doubt higher now. But it was not possible to reprint it without additions. When it was issued in 1891 Ibsen was still alive, and had not yet produced The Master Builder, or Little Eyolf, or John Gabriel Borkman, or When We Dead Awaken. Without an account of these four final masterpieces, a book entitled The Quintessence of Ibsenism would have been a fraud on its purchasers; and it was the difficulty of finding time to write the additional chapters on these plays, and review Ibsen's position from the point of view reached when his work ended with his death and his canonization as an admitted grand master of European literature, that has prevented me for twenty years from complying with the demand for a second edition. Also, perhaps, some relics of my old, or rather my young conscience, which revolted against hasty work. Now that my own stream is nearer the sea, I am more inclined to encourage myself in haste and recklessness by reminding myself that *le mieux est l'ennemi du bien*, and that I had better cobble up a new edition as best I can than not supply it at all.

I have taken all possible precautions to keep the reader's mind free from verbal confusion in following Ibsen's attack on ideals and idealism, a confusion that might have been avoided could his plays, without losing the naturalness of their dialogue, have been translated into the language of the English Bible. It is not too much to say that the works of Ibsen furnish one of the best modern keys to the prophecies of Scripture. Read the prophets, major and minor, from Isaiah to Malachi, without such a key, and you will be puzzled and bored by the almost continuous protest against and denunciation of idolatry and prostitution. Simpletons read all this passionate invective with sleepy unconcern, concluding thoughtlessly that idolatry means praying to stocks and stones instead of to brass lectern eagles and the new reredos presented by the local distiller in search of a title; and as to prostitution, they think of it as "the social evil," and regret that the translators of the Bible used a much blunter word. But nobody who has ever heard real live men talking about graven images and traders in sex can for a moment suppose them to be the things the prophets denounced so earnestly. For idols and idolatry read ideals and idealism; for the prostitution of Piccadilly Circus read not only the prostitution of the journalist, the political lawyer, the parson selling his soul to the squire, the ambitious politician selling his soul for office, but the much more intimate and widespread idolatries and

prostitutions of the private snob, the domestic tyrant
and voluptuary, and the industrial adventurer. At once
the prophetic warnings and curses take on meaning
and proportion, and lose that air of exaggerated
righteousness and tiresome conventional rant which
repels readers who do not possess Ibsen's clue. I have
sometimes thought of reversing the operation, and
substituting in this book the words idol and idolatry
for ideal and idealism; but it would be impossible without spoiling the actuality of Ibsen's criticism of society.
If you call a man a rascally idealist, he is not only
shocked and indignant but puzzled: in which condition you can rely on his attention. If you call him a
rascally idolater, he concludes calmly that you do not
know that he is a member of the Church of England.
I have therefore left the old wording. Save for certain
adaptations made necessary by the lapse of time and
the hand of death, the book stands as it did, with a
few elucidations which I might have made in 1891
had I given the text a couple of extra revisions. Also,
of course, the section dealing with the last four plays.
The two concluding chapters are new. There is no
fundamental change: above all, no dilution.

Whether this edition will change people's minds to
the extent to which the first did (to my own great
astonishment) I do not know. In the eighteen-nineties
one jested about the revolt of the daughters, and of
the wives who slammed the front door like Nora. At
present the revolt has become so general that even the
feeblest and oldest after-dinner jesters dare no longer
keep Votes for Women on their list of stale pleasantries
about mothers-in-law, rational dress, and mixed bathing.
Men are waking up to the perception that in killing
women's souls they have killed their own. Mr.
Granville-Barker's worthy father of six unmarriage-
able daughters in The Madras House, ruefully exclaiming, "It seems to me I've been made a convenience of
all my life," has taken away the excited attention that

Nora once commanded when she said, "I have been living all these years with a strange man." When she meets Helmer's "No man sacrifices his honor for a woman" with her "Thousands of women have done that for men," there is no longer the old impressed assent: men fiercely protest that it is not true; that, on the contrary, for every woman who has sacrificed her honor for a man's sake, ten men have sacrificed their honor for a woman's. In the plays of Gorki and Tchekov, against which all the imbecilities and outrages of the old anti-Ibsen campaign are being revived (for the Press never learns anything by experience), the men appear as more tragically sacrificed by evil social conditions and their romantic and idealistic disguises than the women. Now it may be that into this new atmosphere my book will come with quite an old-fashioned air. As I write these lines the terrible play with which Strindberg wreaked the revenge of the male for A Doll's House has just been performed for the first time in London under the title of Creditors. In that, as in Brieux's Les Hannetons, it is the man who is the victim of domesticity, and the woman who is the tyrant and soul destroyer. Thus A Doll's House did not dispose of the question: it only brought on the stage the endless recriminations of idealistic marriage. And how has Strindberg, Ibsen's twin giant, been received? With an even idler stupidity than Ibsen himself, because Ibsen appealed to the rising energy of the revolt of women against idealism; but Strindberg attacks women ruthlessly, trying to rouse men from the sloth and sensuality of their idealized addiction to them; and as the men, unlike the women, do not want to be roused, whilst the women do not like to be attacked, there is no conscious Strindberg movement to relieve the indifference, the dull belittlement, the spiteful hostility against which the devotees of Ibsen fought so slashingly in the nineties. But the unconscious movement is violent enough. As I write, it is only two days since an eminent bacteriologist filled three columns of The Times with a wild Strindbergian letter in which he declared that women must be politically and professionally secluded and indeed excluded, because their presence and influence inflict on men an obsession so disabling and dangerous that men and women can work together or legislate together only on the same conditions as horses and mares: that is, by the surgical destruction of the male's sex. The Times and The Pall Mall Gazette gravely accept this outburst as "scientific," and heartily endorse it; though only a few weeks have elapsed since The Times dismissed Strindberg's play and Strindberg himself with curt superciliousness as uninteresting and negligible. Not many years ago, a performance of a play by myself, the action of which was placed in an imaginary Ibsen Club, in which the comedy of the bewilderment of conventional people when brought suddenly into contact with the Ibsenist movement (both understood and misunderstood) formed the atmosphere of the piece, was criticized in terms which shewed that our critics are just as hopelessly in the rear of Ibsen as they were in 1891. The only difference was that whereas in 1891 they would have insulted Ibsen, they now accept him as a classic. But understanding of the change of mind produced by Ibsen, or notion that they live in a world which is seething with the reaction of Ibsen's ideas against the ideas of Sardou and Tom Taylor, they have none. They stare with equal unintelligence at the sieges and stormings of separate homesteads by Ibsen or Strindberg, and at the attack all along the front of refined society into which these sieges and stormings have now developed. Whether the attack is exquisite, touching, delicate, as in Tchekov's Cherry Orchard, Galsworthy's Silver Box, and Granville-Barker's Anne Leete, or ruthless, with every trick of intellectual ruffianism and ribaldry, and every engine of dramatic controversy, there is the same pettish disappointment at the absence of the old conventions, the same gaping unconsciousness of the meaning and purpose of the warfare in which each play is a battle, as in the days when this book was new.

Our political journalists are even blinder than our artistic ones in this matter. The credit of our domestic ideals having been shaken to their foundations, as through a couple of earthquake shocks, by Ibsen and Strindberg (the Arch-Individualists of the nineteenth century) whilst the Socialists have been idealizing, sentimentalizing, denouncing Capitalism for sacrificing Love and Home and Domestic Happiness and Children and Duty to money, greed and ambition, yet it remains a commonplace of political journalism to assume that Socialism is the deadliest enemy of the domestic ideals and Unsocialism their only hope and refuge. In the same breath the world-grasping commercial synthesis we call Capitalism, built up by generations of Scotch Rationalists and English Utilitarians, Atheists, Agnostics and Natural-Selectionists, with Malthus as the one churchman among all its prophets, is proclaimed the bulwark of the Christian Churches. We used to be told that the people that walked in darkness have seen a great light. When our people see the heavens blazing with suns, they simply keep their eyes shut, and walk on in darkness until they have led us into the pit. No matter: I am not a domestic idealist; and it pleases me to think that the Life Force may have providential aims in thus keeping my opponents off the trail.

But for all that I must not darken counsel. I therefore, without further apology, launch my old torpedo with the old charge in it, leaving to the new chapters at the end what I have to say about the change in the theatre since Ibsen set his potent leaven to work there.

AYOT ST. LAWRENCE, 1912-13.

PREFACE TO THE FIRST EDITION

IN THE spring of 1890, the Fabian Society, finding itself at a loss for a course of lectures to occupy its summer meetings, was compelled to make shift with a series of papers put forward under the general heading of Socialism in Contemporary Literature. The Fabian Essayists, strongly pressed to do "something or other," for the most part shook their heads; but in the end Sydney Olivier consented to "take Zola"; I consented to "take Ibsen"; and Hubert Bland undertook to read all the Socialist novels of the day, an enterprise the desperate failure of which resulted in the most amusing paper of the series. William Morris, asked to read a paper on himself, flatly declined, but gave us one on Gothic Architecture. Stepniak also came to the rescue with a lecture on modern Russian fiction; and so the Society tided over the summer without having to close its doors, but also without having added anything whatever to the general stock of information on Socialism in Contemporary Literature. After this I cannot claim that my paper on Ibsen, which was duly read at the St. James's Restaurant on the 18th July 1890, under the presidency of Mrs. Annie Besant, and which was the first form of this little book, is an original work in the sense of being the result of a spontaneous internal impulse on my part. Having purposely couched it in the most provocative terms (of which traces may be found by the curious in its present state), I did not attach much importance to the somewhat lively debate that arose upon it; and I had laid it aside as a *pièce d'occasion* which had served its turn, when the production of Rosmersholm at the Vaudeville Theatre by Florence Farr, the inauguration of the Independent Theatre by Mr. J. T. Grein with a performance of Ghosts, and the sensation created by the experiment of Elizabeth Robins and Marion Lea with Hedda Gabler, started a frantic newspaper controversy, in which I could see no sign of any of the disputants having ever been forced by circumstances, as I had, to make up his mind definitely as to what Ibsen's plays meant, and to defend his view face to face with some of the keenest debaters in London. I allow due weight to the fact that Ibsen himself has not enjoyed this Fabian advantage; but I have also shewn that the existence of a discoverable and perfectly definite thesis in a poet's work by no means depends on the completeness of his own intellectual consciousness of it. At any rate, the controversialists, whether in the abusive stage, or the apologetic stage, or the hero-worshipping stage, by no means made clear what they were abusing, or apologizing for, or going into ecstasies about; and I came to the conclusion that my explanation might as well be placed in the field until a better could be found.

With this account of the origin of the book, and a reminder that it is not a critical essay on the poetic beauties of Ibsen, but simply an exposition of Ibsenism, I offer it to my readers to make what they can of.

LONDON, June 1891.

The Quintessence of Ibsenism
NOW COMPLETED TO THE DEATH OF IBSEN

THE TWO PIONEERS

THAT is, pioneers of the march to the plains of heaven (so to speak).

The second, whose eyes are in the back of his head, is the man who declares that it is wrong to do something that no one has hitherto seen any harm in.

The first, whose eyes are very longsighted and in the usual place, is the man who declares that it is right to do something hitherto regarded as infamous.

The second is treated with great respect by the army. They give him testimonials; name him the Good man; and hate him like the devil.

The first is stoned and shrieked at by the whole army. They call him all manner of opprobrious names; grudge him his bare bread and water; and secretly adore him as their savior from utter despair.

Let me take an example from life of my pioneers. Shelley was a pioneer and nothing else: he did both first and second pioneer's work.

Now compare the effect produced by Shelley as abstinence preacher or second pioneer with that which he produced as indulgence preacher or first pioneer. For example:

SECOND PIONEER PROPOSITION: It is wrong to kill animals and eat them.

FIRST PIONEER PROPOSITION: It is not wrong to take your sister as your wife.[1]

Here the second pioneer appears as a gentle humanitarian, and the first as an unnatural corrupter of public morals and family life. So much easier is it to declare the right wrong than the wrong right in a society with a guilty conscience, to which, as to Dickens's detective, "Any possible move is a probable move provided it's in a wrong direction." Just as the liar's punishment is, not in the least that he is not believed, but that he cannot believe any one else; so a guilty society can more easily be persuaded that any ap-

[1] The curious persistence of this proposition in the higher poetry of the nineteenth century is not easy to account for now that it sounds both unimportant and old-fashioned. It is as if one said "It is not wrong to stand on one's head." The reply is "You may be very right; but as nobody wants to, why bother about it?" Yet I think this sensible way of treating the matter—obviously more healthy than the old morbid horror—has been produced largely by the refusal of poets like Shelley and Wagner to accept the theory of natural antipathy as the basis of the tables of Consanguinity, and by the subsequent publication of masses of evidence by sociologists, from Herbert Spencer to Westermarck, shewing that such tables are entirely conventional and that all our prohibitions have been either ignored or actually turned into positive obligations at one time or another without any shock to human instincts. The consequence is that our eyes are now opened to the practical social reasons for barring marriage between Laon and Cythna, Siegmund and Sieglinda; and the preaching of incest as something poetic in itself has lost all its morbid interest and ceased. Also we are beginning to recognize the important fact that the absence of romantic illusion as between persons brought up together, which undoubtedly exists, and which used to be mistaken for natural antipathy, cannot be depended on as between strangers, however close their consanguinity, and that any domestic or educational system which segregates the sexes produces romantic illusion, no matter how undesirable it may be. It will be seen later on in the chapter dealing with the play called Ghosts, that Ibsen took this modern view that consanguinity does not count between strangers. I have accepted it myself in my play Mrs. Warren's Profession. (1912.)

parently innocent act is guilty than that any apparently
guilty act is innocent.

The English newspaper which best represented the
guilty conscience of the middle class, was, when Ibsen's
plays reached England, The Daily Telegraph. If we
can find that The Daily Telegraph attacked Ibsen as
The Quarterly Review used to attack Shelley, it will
occur to us at once that there must be something of
the first pioneer about Ibsen.

The late Clement Scott, at that time dramatic critic
to The Daily Telegraph, was a sentimentally good-
natured gentleman, not then a pioneer, though he had
in his time fought hard for the advance in British
drama represented by the plays of Robertson. He was
also an emotional, impressionable, zealous, and sincere
Roman Catholic. He accused Ibsen of dramatic im-
potence, ludicrous amateurishness, nastiness, vulgarity,
egotism, coarseness, absurdity, uninteresting verbosity,
and "suburbanity," declaring that he has taken ideas
that would have inspired a great tragic poet, and
vulgarized and debased them in dull, hateful, loathsome, horrible plays. This criticism, which occurs in
a notice of the first performance of Ghosts in England,
is to be found in The Daily Telegraph for the 14th
March 1891, and is supplemented by a leading article
which compares the play to an open drain, a loathsome sore unbandaged, a dirty act done publicly, or
a lazar house with all its doors and windows open.
Bestial, cynical, disgusting, poisonous, sickly, delirious,
indecent, loathsome, fetid, literary carrion, crapulous
stuff, clinical confessions: all these epithets are used in
the article as descriptive of Ibsen's work. "Realism,"
said the writer, "is one thing; but the nostrils of the audience must not be visibly held before a play can be
stamped as true to nature. It is difficult to expose in
decorous words the gross and almost putrid indecorum
of this play." As the performance of Ghosts took

place on the evening of the 13th March, and the criticism appeared next morning, it is evident that Clement Scott must have gone straight from the theatre to the newspaper office, and there, in an almost hysterical condition, penned his share of this extraordinary protest. The literary workmanship bears marks of haste and disorder, which, however, only heighten the expression of the passionate horror produced in the writer by seeing Ghosts on the stage. He calls on the authorities to cancel the license of the theatre, and declares that he has been exhorted to laugh at honor, to disbelieve in love, to mock at virtue, to distrust friendship, and to deride fidelity.

If this document were at all singular, it would rank as one of the curiosities of criticism, exhibiting, as it does, the most seasoned playgoer in London thrown into convulsions by a performance which was witnessed with approval, and even with enthusiasm, by many persons of approved moral and artistic conscientiousness. But Clement Scott's criticism was hardly distinguishable in tone from dozens of others which appeared simultaneously. His opinion was the vulgar opinion. Mr. Alfred Watson, critic to The Standard, the leading Tory daily paper, proposed that proceedings should be taken against the theatre under Lord Campbell's Act for the suppression of disorderly houses. Clearly Clement Scott and his editor Sir Edwin Arnold, with whom rested the final responsibility for the article which accompanied the criticism, represented a considerable party.

How then is it that Ibsen, a Norwegian playwright of European celebrity, attracted one section of the English people so strongly that they hailed him as the greatest living dramatic poet and moral teacher, whilst another section was so revolted by his works that they described him in terms which they themselves admitted to be, by the necessities of the case, all but obscene? This phenomenon, which has occurred throughout

Europe whenever Ibsen's plays have been acted, as well as in America and Australia, must be exhaustively explained before the plays can be described without danger of reproducing the same confusion in the reader's own mind. Such an explanation, therefore, must be my first business.

Understand, at the outset, that the explanation will not be an explaining away. Clement Scott's judgment did not mislead him in the least as to Ibsen's meaning. Ibsen means all that most revolted his critic. For example, in Ghosts, the play in question, a clergyman and a married woman fall in love with one another. The woman proposes to abandon her husband and live with the clergyman. He recalls her to duty, and makes her behave as a virtuous woman. She afterwards tells him that this was a crime on his part. Ibsen agrees with her, and has written the play to bring you round to his opinion. Clement Scott did not agree with her, and believed that when you are brought round to her opinion you have been morally corrupted. By this conviction he was impelled to denounce Ibsen as he did, Ibsen being equally impelled to propagate the convictions which provoked the attack. Which of the two is right cannot be decided until it is ascertained whether a society of persons holding Ibsen's opinions would be higher or lower than a society holding Clement Scott's.

There are many people who cannot conceive this as an open question. To them a denunciation of any recognized practices is an incitement to unsocial conduct; and every utterance in which an assumption of the eternal validity of these practices is not implicit is a paradox. Yet all progress involves the beating of them from that position. By way of illustration, one may rake up the case of Proudhon, who in the year 1840 carefully defined property as theft. This was thought the very maddest paradox that ever man hazarded: it seemed obvious that a society which coun-

tenanced such a proposition must speedily be reduced
to the condition of a sacked city. Today schemes for
the confiscation by taxation and supertaxation of min-
ing royalties and ground rents are commonplaces of
social reform; and the honesty of the relation of our
big property holders to the rest of the community is
challenged on all hands. It would be easy to multiply
instances, though the most complete are now inef-
fective through the triumph of the original paradox
having obliterated all memory of the opposition it
first had to encounter. The point to seize is that social
progress takes effect through the replacement of old
institutions by new ones; and since every institution
involves the recognition of the duty of conforming to
it, progress must involve the repudiation of an established duty at every step. If the Englishman had
not repudiated the duty of absolute obedience to his
king, his political progress would have been impossible.
If women had not repudiated the duty of absolute
submission to their husbands, and defied public opinion
as to the limits set by modesty to their education, they
would never have gained the protection of the Married
Women's Property Act, the municipal vote, or the
power to qualify themselves as medical practitioners.
If Luther had not trampled on his duty to the head of
his Church and on his vow of chastity, our clergy
would still have to choose between celibacy and prof-
ligacy. There is nothing new, then, in the defiance of
duty by the reformer: every step of progress means
a duty repudiated, and a scripture torn up. And every
reformer is denounced accordingly: Luther as an
apostate, Cromwell as a traitor, Mary Wollstonecraft
as an unwomanly virago, Shelley as a libertine, and
Ibsen as all the things enumerated in The Daily Telegraph.

This crablike progress of social evolution, in which
the individual advances by seeming to go backward,
continues to illude us in spite of all the lessons of

history. To the pious man the newly made freethinker, suddenly renouncing supernatural revelation, and denying all obligation to believe the Bible and obey the commandments as such, appears to be claiming the right to rob and murder at large. But the free-thinker soon finds reasons for not doing what he does not want to do; and these reasons seem to him to be far more binding on our conscience than the precepts of a book of which the infallibility cannot be rationally proved. The pious man is at last forced to admit—as he was in the case of the late Charles Bradlaugh, for instance—that the disciples of Voltaire and Tom Paine do not pick pockets or cut throats oftener than your even Christian: he actually is driven to doubt whether Voltaire himself (poor Voltaire, who built a church, and was the greatest philanthropist of his time!) really screamed and saw the devil on his deathbed.

This experience by no means saves the rationalist[2] from falling into the same conservatism when the time comes for his own belief to be questioned. No sooner has he triumphed over the theologian than he forth-with sets up as binding on all men the duty of acting logically with the object of securing the greatest good of the greatest number, with the result that he is pres-ently landed in vivisection, Contagious Diseases Acts, dynamite conspiracies, and other grotesque but strictly reasonable abominations. Reason becomes Dagon, Moloch, and Jehovah rolled into one. Its devotees exult in having freed themselves from the old slavery to a collection of books written by Jewish men of letters. To worship such books was, they can prove, as absurd as to worship sonatas composed by German musicians, as was done by the hero of Wagner's novel-ette, who sat up on his deathbed to say his creed, beginning, "I believe in God, Mozart, and Beethoven."

[2] I had better here warn students of philosophy that I am speaking of rationalism, not as classified in the books, but as apparent in men.

The Voltairean freethinker despises such a piece of sentiment; but is it not much more sensible to worship a sonata constructed by a musician than to worship a syllogism constructed by a logician, since the sonata may encourage heroism, or at least inspire feelings of awe and devotion? This does not occur to the votary of reason; and the rationalist's freethinking soon comes to mean syllogism worship with rites of human sacrifice; for just as the rationalist's pious predecessor thought that the man who scoffed at baptism and the Bible must infallibly yield without resistance to all his criminal propensities, so the rationalist in turn becomes convinced that when a man once loses his faith in vaccination and in Herbert Spencer's Data of Ethics, he is no longer to be trusted to keep his hands off his neighbor's person, purse, or wife.

In process of time the age of reason had to go its way after the age of faith. In actual experience, the first shock to rationalism comes from the observation that though nothing can persuade women to adopt it, their impatience of reasoning no more prevents them from arriving at right conclusions than the masculine belief in it (never a very deeply rooted faith in England, by the way, whatever it may have been in France or Greece) saves men from arriving at wrong ones. When this generalization has to be modified in view of the fact that some women are beginning to try their skill at ratiocination, reason is not re-established on the throne; because the result of Woman's reasoning is that she begins to fall into all the errors which men are just learning to mistrust. The moment she sets about doing things for reasons instead of merely finding reasons for what she wants to do, there is no saying what mischief she will be at next: there being just as good reasons for burning a heretic at the stake as for rescuing a shipwrecked crew from drowning: in fact, there are better.

One of the first and most famous utterances of

rationalism would have condemned it without further hearing had its full significance been seen at the time. Voltaire, taking exception to the trash of some poetaster, was met with the plea "One must live." "I dont see the necessity," replied Voltaire. The evasion was worthy of the Father of Lies himself; for Voltaire was face to face with the very necessity he was denying; must have known, consciously or not, that it is the universal postulate; would have understood, if he had lived today, that since all valid human institutions are constructed to fulfil man's will, and his will is to live even when his reason teaches him to die, logical necessity, which was the sort Voltaire meant (the other sort being visible enough) can never be a motor in human action, and is, in short, not necessity at all. But that was not brought to light in Voltaire's time; and he died impenitent, bequeathing to his disciples that most logical of agents, the guillotine, which also "did not see the necessity."

In our own century the recognition of the will as distinct from the reasoning machinery began to spread. Schopenhauer was the first among the moderns[3] to appreciate the enormous practical importance of the distinction, and to make it clear to amateur meta-

[3] I say the moderns, because the will is our old friend the soul or spirit of man; and the doctrine of justification, not by works, but by faith, clearly derives its validity from the consideration that no action, taken apart from the will behind it, has any moral character: for example, the acts which make the murderer and incendiary infamous are exactly similar to those which make the patriotic hero famous. "Original sin" is the will doing mischief. "Divine grace" is the will doing good. Our fathers, unversed in the Hegelian dialectic, could not conceive that these two, each the negation of the other, were the same. Schopenhauer's philosophy, like that of all pessimists, is really based on the old view of the will as original sin, and on the 1750-1850 view that the intellect is the divine grace that is to save us from it. It is as well to warn those who fancy that Schopenhauerism is one and indivisible, that acceptance of its metaphysics by no means involves endorsement of its philosophy.

physicians by concrete instances. Out of his teaching came the formulation of the dilemma Voltaire had shut his eyes to. Here it is. Rationally considered, life is only worth living when its pleasures are greater than its pains. Now to a generation which has ceased to believe in heaven, and has not yet learned that the degradation by poverty of four out of every five of its number is artificial and remediable, the fact that life is not rationally worth living is obvious. It is useless to pretend that the pessimism of Koheleth, Shakespear, Dryden, and Swift can be refuted if the world progresses solely by the destruction of the unfit, and yet can only maintain its civilization by manufacturing the unfit in swarms of which that appalling proportion of four to one represents but the comparatively fit survivors. Plainly then, the reasonable thing for the rationalists to do is to refuse to live. But as none of them will commit suicide in obedience to this demonstration of "the necessity" for it, there is an end of the notion that we live for reasons instead of in fulfilment of our will to live. Thus we are landed afresh in mystery; for positive science gives no account whatever of this will to live. Positive science has dazzled us for nearly a century with its analyses of the machinery of sensation. Its researches into the nature of sound and the construction of the ear, the nature of light and the construction of the eye, its measurement of the speed of sensation, its localization of the functions of the brain, and its hints as to the possibility of producing a homunculus presently as the fruit of its chemical investigation of protoplasm have satisfied the souls of our atheists as completely as belief in divine omniscience and scriptural revelation satisfied the souls of their pious fathers. The fact remains that when Young, Helmholtz, Darwin, Haeckel, and the rest, popularized here among the literate classes by Tyndall and Huxley, and among the proletariat by the lectures of the National Secular Society, have taught you all they know, you are still as utterly at a loss to explain the fact of consciousness as you would have been in the days when you were instructed from The Child's Guide to Knowledge. Materialism, in short, only isolated the great mystery of consciousness by clearing away several petty mysteries with which we had confused it; just as Rationalism isolated the great mystery of the will to live. The isolation made both more conspicuous than before. We thought we had escaped for ever from the cloudy region of metaphysics; and we were only carried further into the heart of them.[4]

We have not yet worn off the strangeness of the position to which we have now been led. Only the other day our highest boast was that we were reasonable human beings. Today we laugh at that conceit, and see ourselves as wilful creatures. Ability to reason accurately is as desirable as ever; for by accurate reasoning only can we calculate our actions so as to do what we intend to do: that is, to fulfil our will; but faith in reason as a prime motor is no longer the criterion of the sound mind, any more than faith in the Bible is the criterion of righteous intention.

At this point, accordingly, the illusion as to the retrogressive movement of progress recurs as strongly as ever. Just as the beneficent step from theology to rationalism seems to the theologist a growth of impiety, does the step from rationalism to the recognition of the will as the prime motor strike the rationalist as a lapse of common sanity; so that to both theologist and

[4] The correlation between Rationalism and Materialism in this process has some immediate practical importance. Those who give up Materialism whilst clinging to Rationalism generally either relapse into abject submission to the most paternal of the Churches, or are caught by the attempts, constantly renewed, of mystics to found a new faith by rationalizing on the hollowness of materialism. The hollowness has nothing in it; and if you have come to grief as a materialist by reasoning about something, you are not likely, as a mystic, to improve matters by reasoning about nothing.

rationalist progress at last appears alarming, threatening, hideous, because it seems to tend towards chaos. The deists Voltaire and Tom Paine were, to the divines of their day, predestined devils, tempting mankind hellward.[5] To deists and divines alike Ferdinand Lassalle, the godless self-worshipper and man-worshipper, would have been a monster. Yet many who today echo Lassalle's demand that economic and political institutions should be adapted to the poor man's will to eat and drink his fill out of the product of the labor he shares, are revolted by Ibsen's acceptance of the impulse towards greater freedom as sufficient ground for the repudiation of any customary duty, however sacred, that conflicts with it. Society, were it even as free as Lassalle's Social-Democratic republic, *must*, it seems to them, go to pieces when conduct is no longer regulated by inviolable covenants.

For what, during all these overthrowings of things sacred and things infallible, has been happening to that pre-eminently sanctified thing, Duty? Evidently it cannot have come off scatheless. First there was man's duty to God, with the priest as assessor. That was repudiated; and then came Man's duty to his neighbor, with Society as the assessor. Will this too be repudiated, and be succeeded by Man's duty to himself, assessed by himself? And if so, what will be the effect on the conception of Duty in the abstract? Let us see.

I have just called Lassalle a self-worshipper. In doing so I cast no reproach on him; for this is the last step in the evolution of the conception of duty. Duty arises

[5] This is not precisely true. Voltaire was what we should now call an advanced Congregationalist: in fact, modern Dissent, on its educated side, is sound Voltaireanism. Voltaire was for some time on very friendly terms with the Genevese pastors. But what with his jests at the expense of Bible worship, and the fact that he could not formally cut himself off from the Established Church of France without placing himself in its power, the pastors had finally to conceal their agreement with him. (1912.)

at first, a gloomy tyranny, out of man's helplessness, his self-mistrust, in a word, his abstract fear. He personifies all that he abstractly fears as God, and straightway becomes the slave of his duty to God. He imposes that slavery fiercely on his children, threatening them with hell, and punishing them for their attempts to be happy. When, becoming bolder, he ceases to fear everything, and dares to love something, this duty of his to what he fears evolves into a sense of duty to what he loves. Sometimes he again personifies what he loves as God; and the God of Wrath becomes the God of Love: sometimes he at once becomes a humanitarian, an altruist, acknowledging only his duty to his neighbor. This stage is correlative to the rationalist stage in the evolution of philosophy and the capitalist phase in the evolution of industry. But in it the emancipated slave of God falls under the dominion of Society, which, having just reached a phase in which all the love is ground out of it by the competitive struggle for money, remorselessly crushes him until, in due course of the further growth of his courage, a sense at last arises in him of his duty to himself. And when this sense is fully grown the tyranny of duty perishes; for now the man's God is his own humanity; and he, self-satisfied at last, ceases to be selfish. The evangelist of this last step must therefore preach the repudiation of duty. This, to the unprepared of his generation, is indeed the wanton masterpiece of paradox. What! after all that has been said by men of noble life as to the secret of all right conduct being only Duty, Duty, Duty, is he to be told how that duty is the primal curse from which we must redeem ourselves before we can advance another step on the road along which, as we imagine (having forgotten the repudiations made by our fathers) duty and duty alone has brought us thus far? But why not? God Almighty was once the most sacred of our conceptions; and he had to be denied. Then Reason became the Infallible Pope, only to be deposed in turn. Is Duty more sacred than God or Reason?

Having now arrived at the prospect of the repudiation of duty by Man, I shall make a digression on the subject of ideals and idealists, as treated by Ibsen. I shall go round in a loop, and come back to the same point by way of the repudiation of duty by Woman; and then at last I shall be in a position to describe Ibsen's plays without risk of misunderstanding.

IDEALS AND IDEALISTS

WE HAVE seen that as Man grows through the ages, he finds himself bolder by the growth of his courage: that is, of his spirit (for so the common people name it), and dares more and more to love and trust instead of to fear and fight. But his courage has other effects: he also raises himself from mere consciousness to knowledge by daring more and more to face facts and tell himself the truth. For in his infancy of helplessness and terror he could not face the inexorable; and facts being of all things the most inexorable, he masked all the threatening ones as fast as he discovered them; so that now every mask requires a hero to tear it off. The king of terrors, Death, was the Arch-Inexorable: Man could not bear the dread of that. He must persuade himself that Death can be propitiated, circumvented, abolished. How he fixed the mask of personal immortality on the face of Death for this purpose we all know. And he did the like with all disagreeables as long as they remained inevitable. Otherwise he must have gone mad with terror of the grim shapes around him, headed by the skeleton with the scythe and hourglass. The masks were his ideals, as he called them; and what, he would ask, would life be without ideals? Thus he became an idealist, and re-

mained so until he dared to begin pulling the masks off
and looking the spectres in the face—dared, that is,
to be more and more a realist. But all men are not
equally brave; and the greatest terror prevailed whenever some realist bolder than the rest laid hands on a
mask which they did not yet dare to do without.

We have plenty of these masks around us still: some
of them more fantastic than any of the Sandwich
islanders' masks in the British Museum. In our novels
and romances especially we see the most beautiful of
all the masks: those devised to disguise the brutalities
of the sexual instinct in the earlier stages of its development, and to soften the rigorous aspect of the iron
laws by which Society regulates its gratification. When
the social organism becomes bent on civilization, it
has to force marriage and family life on the individual,
because it can perpetuate itself in no other way whilst
love is still known only by fitful glimpses, the basis
of sexual relationship being in the main mere physical
appetite. Under these circumstances men try to graft
pleasure on necessity by desperately pretending that
the institution forced upon them is a congenial one,
making it a point of public decency to assume always
that men spontaneously love their kindred better than
their chance acquaintances, and that the woman once
desired is always desired: also that the family is
woman's proper sphere, and that no really womanly
woman ever forms an attachment, or even knows what
it means, until she is requested to do so by a man. Now
if anyone's childhood has been embittered by the
dislike of his mother and the ill-temper of his father;
if his wife has ceased to care for him and he is heartily
tired of his wife; if his brother is going to law with
him over the division of the family property, and his
son acting in studied defiance of his plans and wishes,
it is hard for him to persuade himself that passion is
eternal and that blood is thicker than water. Yet if he

tells himself the truth, all his life seems a waste and a failure by the light of it. It comes then to this, that his neighbors must either agree with him that the whole system is a mistake, and discard it for a new one, which cannot possibly happen until social organization so far outgrows the institution that Society can perpetuate itself without it; or else they must keep him in countenance by resolutely making believe that all the illusions with which it has been masked are realities.

For the sake of precision, let us imagine a community of a thousand persons, organized for the perpetuation of the species on the basis of the British family as we know it at present. Seven hundred of them, we will suppose, find the British family arrangement quite good enough for them. Two hundred and ninety-nine find it a failure, but must put up with it since they are in a minority. The remaining person occupies a position to be explained presently. The 299 failures will not have the courage to face the fact that they are irremediable failures, since they cannot prevent the 700 satisfied ones from coercing them into conformity with the marriage law. They will accordingly try to persuade themselves that, whatever their own particular domestic arrangements may be, the family is a beautiful and holy natural institution. For the fox not only declares that the grapes he cannot get are sour: he also insists that the sloes he *can* get are sweet. Now observe what has happened. The family as it really is is a conventional arrangement, legally enforced, which the majority, because it happens to suit them, think good enough for the minority, whom it happens not to suit at all. The family as a beautiful and holy natural institution is only a fancy picture of what every family would have to be if everybody was to be suited, invented by the minority as a mask for the reality, which in its nakedness is intolerable to them. We call this sort of fancy picture an Ideal; and the policy of forcing individuals to act on the assumption that all ideals are real, and to recognize and accept such action as standard moral conduct, absolutely valid under all circumstances, contrary conduct or any advocacy of it being discountenanced and punished as immoral, may therefore be described as the policy of Idealism. Our 299 domestic failures are therefore become idealists as to marriage; and in proclaiming the ideal in fiction, poetry, pulpit and platform oratory, and serious private conversation, they will far outdo the 700 who comfortably accept marriage as a matter of course, never dreaming of calling it an "institution," much less a holy and beautiful one, and being pretty plainly of opinion that Idealism is a crackbrained fuss about nothing. The idealists, hurt by this, will retort by calling them Philistines. We then have our society classified as 700 Philistines and 299 idealists, leaving one man unclassified: the man strong enough to face the truth the idealists are shirking.

Such a man says of marriage, "This thing is a failure for many of us. It is insufferable that two human beings, having entered into relations which only warm affection can render tolerable, should be forced to maintain them after such affections have ceased to exist, or in spite of the fact that they have never arisen. The alleged natural attractions and repulsions upon which the family ideal is based do not exist; and it is historically false that the family was founded for the purpose of satisfying them. Let us provide otherwise for the social ends which the family subserves, and then abolish its compulsory character altogether." What will be the attitude of the rest to this outspoken man? The Philistines will simply think him mad. But the idealists will be terrified beyond measure at the proclamation of their hidden thought—at the presence of the traitor among the conspirators of silence—at the rending of the beautiful veil they and their poets have

woven to hide the unbearable face of the truth. They
will crucify him, burn him, violate their own ideals
of family affection by taking his children away from
him, ostracize him, brand him as immoral, profligate,
filthy, and appeal against him to the despised Philistines, specially idealized for the occasion as Society.
How far they will proceed against him depends on
how far his courage exceeds theirs. At his worst, they
call him cynic and paradoxer: at his best they do their
utmost to ruin him if not to take his life. Thus, pur-
blindly courageous moralists like Mandeville and La-
rochefoucauld, who merely state unpleasant facts without denying the validity of current ideals, and who
indeed depend on those ideals to make their statements
piquant, get off with nothing worse than this name of
cynic, the free use of which is a familiar mark of the
zealous idealist. But take the case of the man who has
already served us as an example: Shelley. The idealists
did not call Shelley a cynic: they called him a fiend
until they invented a new illusion to enable them to
enjoy the beauty of his lyrics, this illusion being
nothing less than the pretence that since he was at
bottom an idealist himself, his ideals must be identical
with those of Tennyson and Longfellow, neither of
whom ever wrote a line in which some highly respectable ideal was not implicit.[1]

[1] The following are examples of the two stages of Shelley
criticism:

"We feel as if one of the darkest of the fiends had been
clothed with a human body to enable him to gratify his enmity
against the human race, and as if the supernatural atrocity of
his hate were only heightened by his power to do injury. So
strongly has this impression dwelt upon our minds that we
absolutely asked a friend, who had seen this individual, to
describe him to us—as if a cloven hoof, or horn, or flames from
the mouth, must have marked the external appearance of so
bitter an enemy of mankind." (Literary Gazette, 19th May
1821.)

"A beautiful and ineffectual angel, beating in the void his

Here the admission that Shelley, the realist, was an idealist too, seems to spoil the whole argument. And it certainly spoils its verbal consistency. For we unfortunately use this word ideal indifferently to denote both the institution which the ideal masks and the mask itself, thereby producing desperate confusion of thought, since the institution may be an effete and poisonous one, whilst the mask may be, and indeed generally is, an image of what we would fain have in its place. If the existing facts, with their masks on, are to be called ideals, and the future possibilities which the masks depict are also to be called ideals—if, again, the man who is defending exisiting institutions by maintaining their identity with their masks is to be confounded under one name with the man who is striving to realize the future possibilities by tearing the mask and the thing masked asunder, then the position cannot be intelligibly described by mortal pen: you and I, reader, will be at cross purposes at every sentence unless you allow me to distinguish pioneers like Shelley and Ibsen as realists from the idealists of my imaginary community of one thousand. If you ask why I have not allotted the terms the other way, and called Shelley and Ibsen idealists and the conventionalists realists, I reply that Ibsen himself, though he has not formally made the distinction, has so repeatedly harped on conventions and conventionalists as ideals and idealists that if I were now perversely to call them realities and realists, I should confuse readers of The Wild Duck and Rosmersholm more than I should help them. Doubtless I shall be reproached for

---

luminous wings in vain." (MATTHEW ARNOLD, in the preface to his selection of poems by Byron, dated 1881.)

The 1881 opinion is much sillier than the 1821 opinion. Further samples will be found in the articles of Henry Salt, one of the few writers on Shelley who understand his true position as a social pioneer.

puzzling people by thus limiting the meaning of the term ideal. But what, I ask, is that inevitable passing perplexity compared to the inextricable tangle I must produce if I follow the custom, and use the word indiscriminately in its two violently incompatible senses? If the term realist is objected to on account of some of its modern associations, I can only recommend you, if you must associate it with something else than my own description of its meaning (I do not deal in definitions), to associate it, not with Zola and Maupassant, but with Plato.

Now let us return to our community of 700 Philistines, 299 idealists, and 1 realist. The mere verbal ambiguity against which I have just provided is as nothing beside that which comes of any attempt to express the relations of these three sections, simple as they are, in terms of the ordinary systems of reason and duty. The idealist, higher in the ascent of evolution than the Philistine, yet hates the highest and strikes at him with a dread and rancor of which the easy-going Philistine is guiltless. The man who has risen above the danger and the fear that his acquisitiveness will lead him to theft, his temper to murder, and his affections to debauchery: this is he who is denounced as an archscoundrel and libertine, and thus confounded with the lowest because he is the highest. And it is not the ignorant and stupid who maintain this error, but the literate and the cultured. When the true prophet speaks, he is proved to be both rascal and idiot, not by those who have never read of how foolishly such learned demonstrations have come off in the past, but by those who have themselves written volumes on the crucifixions, the burnings, the stonings, the headings and hangings, the Siberia transportations, the calumny and ostracism which have been the lot of the pioneer as well as of the camp follower. It is from men of established literary reputation that we learn that

William Blake was mad, that Shelley was spoiled by living in a low set, that Robert Owen was a man who did not know the world, that Ruskin was incapable of comprehending political economy, that Zola was a mere blackguard, and that Ibsen was "a Zola with a wooden leg." The great musician, accepted by the unskilled listener, is vilified by his fellow-musicians: it was the musical culture of Europe that pronounced Wagner the inferior of Mendelssohn and Meyerbeer. The great artist finds his foes among the painters, and not among the men in the street: it was the Royal Academy which placed forgotten nobodies above Burne Jones. It is not rational that it should be so; but it is so, for all that.

The realist at last loses patience with ideals altogether, and sees in them only something to blind us, something to numb us, something to murder self in us, something whereby, instead of resisting death, we can disarm it by committing suicide. The idealist, who has taken refuge with the ideals because he hates himself and is ashamed of himself, thinks that all this is so much the better. The realist, who has come to have a deep respect for himself and faith in the validity of his own will, thinks it so much the worse. To the one, human nature, naturally corrupt, is held back from ruinous excesses only by self-denying conformity to the ideals. To the other these ideals are only swaddling clothes which man has outgrown, and which insufferably impede his movements. No wonder the two cannot agree. The idealist says, "Realism means egotism; and egotism means depravity." The realist declares that when a man abnegates the will to live and be free in a world of the living and free, seeking only to conform to ideals for the sake of being, not himself, but "a good man," then he is morally dead and rotten, and must be left unheeded to abide his resurrection, if that by good

cf. Hulme on "romantic" vs. "classicist".

luck arrive before his bodily death.[2] Unfortunately, this is the sort of speech that nobody but a realist understands. It will be more amusing as well as more convincing to take an actual example of an idealist criticizing a realist.

[2] The above was written in 1890, ten years before Ibsen, in When We Dead Awaken, fully adopted its metaphor without, as far as I know, having any knowledge of my essay. Such an anticipation is a better proof than any mere argument that I found the right track of Ibsen's thought. (1912.)

THE WOMANLY WOMAN

In 1890 the literary sensation of the day was the Diary of Marie Bashkirtseff. An outline of it, with a running commentary, was given in The Review of Reviews (June 1890) by the editor, the late William Stead, who, having gained an immense following by a public service in rendering which he had to simulate a felony and suffer imprisonment for it in order to prove that it was possible, was engaged in a campaign with the object of establishing the ideal of sexual "purity" as a condition of public life. He had certain Ibsenist qualities: faith in himself, wilfulness, conscientious unscrupulousness, and could always make himself heard. Prominent among his ideals was an ideal of womanliness. In support of that ideal he would, like all idealists, make and believe any statement, however obviously and grotesquely unreal. When he found Marie Bashkirtseff's account of herself utterly incompatible with the picture of a woman's mind presented to him by his ideal, he was confronted with the dilemma that either Marie was not a woman or else his ideal was false to nature. He actually accepted the former alternative. "Of the distinctively womanly," he says, "there is in her but little trace. She was the very antithesis of a true woman." William's next difficulty was, that self-control, being a leading quality in his ideal, could not have been possessed by Marie: otherwise she would

have been more like his ideal. Nevertheless he had to
record that she, without any compulsion from circumstances, made herself a highly skilled artist by working
ten hours a day for six years. Let anyone who thinks
that this is no evidence of self-control just try it for
six months. William's verdict nevertheless was "No
self-control." However, his fundamental quarrel with
Marie came out in the following lines. "Marie," he
said, "was artist, musician, wit, philosopher, student,
anything you like but a natural woman with a heart to
love, and a soul to find its supreme satisfaction in sacrifice for lover or for child." Now of all the idealist
abominations that make society pestiferous, I doubt if
there be any so mean as that of forcing self-sacrifice on
a woman under pretence that she likes it; and, if she
ventures to contradict the pretence, declaring her no
true woman. In India they carried this piece of idealism
to the length of declaring that a wife could not bear to
survive her husband, but would be prompted by her
own faithful, loving, beautiful nature to offer up her
life on the pyre which consumed his dead body. The
astonishing thing is that women, sooner than be branded
as unsexed wretches, allowed themselves to be stupe-
fied with drink, and in that unwomanly condition burnt
alive. British Philistinism put down widow idealizing
with the strong hand; and suttee is abolished in India.
The English form of it still flourishes; and Stead, the
rescuer of the children,[1] was one of its high priests.
Imagine his feelings on coming across this entry in a
woman's diary: "I love myself." Or this, "I swear
solemnly—by the Gospels, by the passion of Christ, by
MYSELF—that in four years I will be famous." The
young woman was positively proposing to exercise
for her own sake all the powers that were given to her,
in Stead's opinion, solely that she might sacrifice them

[1] It was to force the Government to take steps to suppress
child prostitution that Stead resorted to the desperate expedient
already alluded to. He succeeded.

for her lover or child! No wonder he was driven to exclaim again, "She was very clever, no doubt; but woman she was not."

Now observe this notable result. Marie Bashkirtseff, instead of being a less agreeable person than the ordinary female conformer to the ideal of womanliness, was most conspicuously the reverse. Stead himself wrote as one infatuated with her mere diary, and pleased himself by representing her as a person who fascinated everybody, and was a source of delight to all about her by the mere exhilaration and hope-giving atmosphere of her wilfulness. The truth is, that in real life a self-sacrificing woman, or, as Stead would have put it, a womanly woman, is not only taken advantage of, but disliked as well for her pains. No man pretends that his soul finds its supreme satisfaction in self-sacrifice: such an affectation would stamp him as coward and weakling: the manly man is he who takes the Bashkirtseff view of himself. But men are not the less loved on this account. No one ever feels helpless by the side of the self-helper; whilst the self-sacrificer is always a drag, a responsibility, a reproach, an everlasting and unnatural trouble with whom no really strong soul can live. Only those who have helped themselves know how to help others, and to respect their right to help themselves.[2]

[2] Shortly after the publication of this passage, a German lady told me that she knew "where I had got it from," evidently not meaning from Ibsen. She added "You have been reading Nietzsche's Through Good and Evil and Out at the other Side." That was the first I ever heard of Nietzsche. I mention this fact, not with the ridiculous object of vindicating my "originality" in nineteenth century fashion, but because I attach great importance to the evidence that the movement voiced by Schopenhauer, Wagner, Ibsen, Nietzsche, and Strindberg, was a world movement, and would have found expression if every one of these writers had perished in his cradle. I have dealt with this question in the preface to my play Major Barbara. The movement is alive today in the philosophy of Bergson and the plays of Gorki, Tchekov, and the post-Ibsen English drama. (1912.)

Although romantic idealists generally insist on self-surrender as an indispensable element in true womanly love, its repulsive effect is well known and feared in practice by both sexes. The extreme instance is the reckless self-abandonment seen in the infatuation of passionate sexual desire. Everyone who becomes the object of that infatuation shrinks from it instinctively. Love loses its charm when it is not free; and whether the compulsion is that of custom and law, or of infatuation, the effect is the same: it becomes valueless and even abhorrent, like the caresses of a maniac. The desire to give inspires no affection unless there is also the power to withhold; and the successful wooer, in both sexes alike, is the one who can stand out for honorable conditions, and, failing them, go without. Such conditions are evidently not offered to either sex by the legal marriage of today; for it is the intense repugnance inspired by the compulsory character of the legalized conjugal relation that leads, first to the idealization of marriage whilst it remains indispensable as a means of perpetuating society; then to its modification by divorce and by the abolition of penalties for refusal to comply with judicial orders for restitution of conjugal rights; and finally to its disuse and disappearance as the responsibility for the maintenance and education of the rising generation is shifted from the parent to the community.[3]

[3] A dissertation on the anomalies and impossibilities of the marriage law at its present stage would be too far out of the main course of my argument to be introduced in the text above; but it may be well to point out in passing to those who regard marriage as an inviolable and inviolate institution, that necessity has already forced us to tamper with it to such an extent that at this moment (1891) the highest court in the kingdom is face to face with a husband and wife, the one demanding whether a woman may saddle him with all the responsibilities of a husband and then refuse to live with him, and the other asking whether the law allows her husband to commit abduction, imprisonment, and rape upon her. If the court says Yes to the husband, indissoluble marriage is made intolerable for men; if it says Yes to the

Although the growing repugnance to face the Church of England marriage service has led many celebrants to omit those passages which frankly explain the object of the institution, we are not likely to dispense with legal ties and obligations, and trust wholly to the permanence of love, until the continuity of society no longer depends on the private nursery. Love, as a practical factor in society, is still a mere appetite. That higher development of it which Ibsen shews us occurring in the case of Rebecca West in Rosmersholm is only known to most of us by the descriptions of great poets, who themselves, as their biographies prove, have known it, not by sustained experience, but only by brief glimpses. Dante loved Beatrice with the higher love; but neither during her life nor after her death was he "faithful" to her or to the woman he actually married. And he would be a bold bourgeois who would pretend to a higher mind than Dante. Tannhäuser may die in the conviction that one moment of the emotion he felt with St. Elizabeth was fuller and happier than all the hours of passion he spent with Venus; but that does not alter the fact that love began for him with Venus, and that its earlier tentatives towards the final goal were attended with relapses. Now Tannhäuser's passion for Venus is a development of the humdrum fondness of the bourgeois Jack for his Jill, a development at once higher and more danger-

---

wife, the position is made intolerable for women; and as this exhausts the possible alternatives, it is clear that provision must be made for the dissolution of such marriages if the institution is to be maintained at all, which it must be until its social function is otherwise provided for. Marriage is thus, by force of circumstances, compelled to buy extension of life by extension of divorce, much as if a fugitive should try to delay a pursuing wolf by throwing portions of his own heart to it. [The court decided against the man; but England still lags behind the rest of Protestant Europe in the necessary readjustment of the law of divorce. See the preface to my play Getting Married, which supplies the dissertation crowded out of the foregoing note. (1912.)

ous, just as idealism is at once higher and more dangerous than Philistinism. The fondness is the germ of the
passion: the passion is the germ of the more perfect
love. When Blake told men that through excess they
would learn moderation, he knew that the way for the
present lay through the Venusberg, and that the race
would assuredly not perish there as some individuals
have, and as the Puritan fears we all shall unless we
find a way round. Also he no doubt foresaw the time
when our children would be born on the other side of
it, and so be spared that fiery purgation.

But the very facts that Blake is still commonly regarded as a crazy visionary, and that the current criticism of Rosmersholm entirely fails even to notice the
evolution of Rebecca's passion for Rosmer into her love
for him, much more to credit the moral transfiguration
which accompanies it, shew how absurd it would be
to pretend, for the sake of edification, that the ordinary
marriage of today is a union between a William Blake
and a Rebecca West, or that it would be possible, even
if it were enlightened policy, to deny the satisfaction
of the sexual appetite to persons who have not reached
that stage. An overwhelming majority of such marriages as are not purely *de convenance* are entered into
for the gratification of that appetite either in its crudest
form or veiled only by those idealistic illusions which
the youthful imagination weaves so wonderfully under
the stimulus of desire, and which older people indul-
gently laugh at.

This being so, it is not surprising that our society,
being directly dominated by men, comes to regard
Woman, not as an end in herself like Man, but solely
as a means of ministering to his appetite. The ideal wife
is one who does everything that the ideal husband likes,
and nothing else. Now to treat a person as a means
instead of an end is to deny that person's right to live.
And to be treated as a means to such an end as sexual

intercourse with those who deny one's right to live is insufferable to any human being. Woman, if she dares face the fact that she is being so treated, must either loathe herself or else rebel. As a rule, when circumstances enable her to rebel successfully—for instance, when the accident of genius enables her to "lose her character" without losing her employment or cutting herself off from the society she values—she does rebel; but circumstances seldom do. Does she then loathe herself? By no means: she deceives herself in the idealist fashion by denying that the love which her suitor offers her is tainted with sexual appetite at all. It is, she declares, a beautiful, disinterested, pure, sublime devotion to another by which a man's life is exalted and purified, and a woman's rendered blest. And of all the cynics, the filthiest to her mind is the one who sees, in the man making honorable proposals to his future wife, nothing but the human male seeking his female. The man himself keeps her confirmed in her illusion; for the truth is unbearable to him too: he wants to form an affectionate tie, and not to drive a degrading bargain. After all, the germ of the highest love is in them both; though as yet it is no more than the appetite they are disguising so carefully from themselves. Consequently every stockbroker who has just brought his business up to marrying point woos in terms of the romantic illusion; and it is agreed between the two that their marriage shall realize the romantic ideal. Then comes the breakdown of the plan. The young wife finds that her husband is neglecting her for his business; that his interests, his activities, his whole life except that one part of it to which only a cynic ever referred before her marriage, lies away from home; and that her business is to sit there and mope until she is wanted. Then what can she do? If she complains, he, the self-helper, can do without her; whilst she is dependent on him for her position, her livelihood, her place in society, her home, her name, her very bread.[4] All this is brought home to her by the first burst of displeasure her complaints provoke. Fortunately, things do not remain for ever at this point: perhaps the most wretched in a woman's life. The self-respect she has lost as a wife she regains as a mother, in which capacity her use and importance to the community compare favorably with those of most men of business. She is wanted in the house, wanted in the market, wanted by the children; and now, instead of weeping because her husband is away in the city, thinking of stocks and shares instead of his ideal woman, she would regard his presence in the house all day as an intolerable nuisance. And so, though she is completely disillusioned on the subject of ideal love, yet, since it has not turned out so badly after all, she countenances the illusion still from the point of view that it is a useful and harmless means of getting boys and girls to marry and settle down. And this conviction is the stronger in her because she feels that if she had known as much about marriage the day before her wedding as she did six months after, it would have been extremely hard to induce her to get married at all.

This prosaic solution is satisfactory only within certain limits. It depends altogether upon the accident of the woman having some natural vocation for domestic management and the care of children, as well as on the husband being fairly good-natured and livable-with. Hence arises the idealist illusion that a vocation for domestic management and the care of children is nat-

---

[4] I should have warned my male readers to be very careful how they presume on this position. In actual practice marriage reduces the man to a greater dependence on the woman than is good for either party. But the woman can tyrannize only by misconduct or threats of misconduct, whilst the man can tyrannize legally, though it must be added that a good deal of the makeshift law that has been set up to restrain this tyranny is very unfair to the man. The writings of Belfort Bax are instructive on this point. (1912.)

ural to women, and that women who lack them are not women at all, but members of the third, or Bashkirtseff sex. Even if this were true, it is obvious that if the Bashkirtseffs are to be allowed to live, they have a right to suitable institutions just as much as men and women. But it is not true. The domestic career is no more natural to all women than the military career is natural to all men; and although in a population emergency it might become necessary for every ablebodied woman to risk her life in childbed just as it might become necessary in a military emergency for every man to risk his life in the battlefield, yet even then it would by no means follow that the child-bearing would endow the mother with domestic aptitudes and capacities as it would endow her with milk. It is of course quite true that the majority of women are kind to children and prefer their own to other people's. But exactly the same thing is true of the majority of men, who nevertheless do not consider that their proper sphere is the nursery. The case may be illustrated more grotesquely by the fact that the majority of women who have dogs are kind to them, and prefer their own dogs to other people's; yet it is not proposed that women should restrict their activities to the rearing of puppies. If we have come to think that the nursery and the kitchen are the natural sphere of a woman, we have done so exactly as English children come to think that a cage is the natural sphere of a parrot: because they have never seen one anywhere else. No doubt there are Philistine parrots who agree with their owners that it is better to be in a cage than out, so long as there is plenty of hempseed and Indian corn there. There may even be idealist parrots who persuade themselves that the mission of a parrot is to minister to the happiness of a private family by whistling and saying Pretty Polly, and that it is in the sacrifice of its liberty to this altruistic pursuit that a true parrot finds the supreme satisfaction of its soul. I will not go so far as to affirm that there are theological parrots who are convinced that imprisonment is the will of God because it is unpleasant; but I am confident that there are rationalist parrots who can demonstrate that it would be a cruel kindness to let a parrot out to fall a prey to cats, or at least to forget its accomplishments and coarsen its naturally delicate fibres in an unprotected struggle for existence. Still, the only parrot a free-souled person can sympathize with is the one that insists on being let out as the first condition of making itself agreeable. A selfish bird, you may say: one that puts its own gratification before that of the family which is so fond of it—before even the greatest happiness of the greatest number: one that, in aping the independent spirit of a man, has unparroted itself and become a creature that has neither the home-loving nature of a bird nor the strength and enterprise of a mastiff. All the same, you respect that parrot in spite of your conclusive reasoning; and if it persists, you will have either to let it out or kill it.

The sum of the matter is that unless Woman repudiates her womanliness, her duty to her husband, to her children, to society, to the law, and to everyone but herself, she cannot emancipate herself. But her duty to herself is no duty at all, since a debt is cancelled when the debtor and creditor are the same person. Its payment is simply a fulfilment of the individual will, upon which all duty is a restriction, founded on the conception of the will as naturally malign and devilish. Therefore Woman has to repudiate duty altogether. In that repudiation lies her freedom; for it is false to say that Woman is now directly the slave of Man: she is the immediate slave of duty; and as man's path to freedom is strewn with the wreckage of the duties and ideals he has trampled on, so must hers be. She may indeed mask her iconoclasm by proving in rationalist fashion, as Man has often done for the sake of a quiet life, that all these discarded idealist conceptions will be fortified instead of shattered by her emancipation. To a person with a turn for logic, such proofs are as easy as playing the piano is to Paderewski. But it will not be true. A whole basketful of ideals of the most sacred quality will be smashed by the achievement of equality for women and men. Those who shrink from such a clatter and breakage may comfort themselves with the reflection that the replacement of the broken goods will be prompt and certain. It is always a case of "The ideal is dead: long live the ideal!" And the advantage of the work of destruction is that every new ideal is less of an illusion than the one it has supplanted; so that the destroyer of ideals, though denounced as an enemy of society, is in fact sweeping the world clear of lies.

My digression is now over. Having traversed my loop as I promised, and come back to Man's repudiation of duty by way of Woman's, I may at last proceed to give some more particular account of Ibsen's work without further preoccupation with Clement Scott's protest, or the many others of which it is the type. For we now see that the pioneer must necessarily provoke such outcry as he repudiates duties, tramples on ideals, profanes what was sacred, sanctifies what was infamous, always driving his plough through gardens of pretty weeds in spite of the laws made against trespassers for the protection of the worms which feed on the roots, always letting in light and air to hasten the putrefaction of decaying matter, and everywhere proclaiming that "the old beauty is no longer beautiful, the new truth no longer true." He can do no less; and what more and what else he does it is not given to all of his generation to understand. And if any man does not understand, and cannot foresee the harvest, what can he do but cry out in all sincerity against such destruction, until at last we come to know the cry of the blind like any other street cry, and to bear with it as an honest cry, albeit a false alarm?

THE AUTOBIOGRAPHICAL
ANTI-IDEALIST EXTRAVAGANZAS

BRAND, 1866

WE ARE now prepared to learn without misgiving that a typical Ibsen play is one in which the leading lady is an unwomanly woman, and the villain an idealist. It follows that the leading lady is not a heroine of the Drury Lane type; nor does the villain forge or assassinate, since he is a villain by virtue of his determination to do nothing wrong. Therefore readers of Ibsen—not playgoers—have sometimes so far misconceived him as to suppose that his villains are examples rather than warnings, and that the mischief and ruin which attend their actions are but the tribulations from which the soul comes out purified as gold from the furnace. In fact, the beginning of Ibsen's European reputation was the edification with which the pious received his great dramatic poem Brand. Brand is not his first play: indeed it is his seventh; and of its six forerunners all are notable and some splendid; but it is in Brand that he definitely, if not yet quite consciously, takes the field against idealism and, like another Luther, nails his thesis to the door of the Temple of Morality. With Brand therefore we must begin, lest we should be swept into an eddy of mere literary criticism, a matter altogether beside the

purpose of this book, which is to distil the quintessence
of Ibsen's message to his age.

Brand the priest is an idealist of heroic earnestness,
strength, and courage. Conventional, comfortable,
sentimental church-going withers into selfish snobbery
and cowardly weakness before his terrible word. "Your
God," he cries, "is an old man: mine is young"; and all
Europe, hearing him, suddenly realizes that it has so
far forgotten God as to worship an image of an elderly
gentleman with a well-trimmed beard, an imposing
forehead, and the expression of a headmaster. Brand,
turning from such idolatrous follies with fierce scorn,
declares himself the champion, not of things as they are,
nor of things as they can be made, but of things as they
ought to be. Things as they ought to be mean for him
things as ordered by men conformed to his ideal of the
perfect Adam, who, again, is not man as he is or can be,
but man conformed to all the ideals: man as it is his
duty to be. In insisting on this conformity, Brand spares
neither himself nor anyone else. Life is nothing: self is
nothing: the perfect Adam is everything. The imperfect Adam does not fall in with these views. A peasant
whom he urges to cross a glacier in a fog because it is
his duty to visit his dying daughter, not only flatly de-
clines, but endeavors forcibly to prevent Brand from
risking his own life. Brand knocks him down, and
sermonizes him with fierce earnestness and scorn. Presently Brand has to cross a fiord in a storm to reach a
dying man who, having committed a series of murders, wants "consolation" from a priest. Brand cannot go
alone: someone must hold the rudder of his boat whilst
he manages the sail. The fisher folk, in whom the old
Adam is strong, do not adopt his estimate of the gravity
of the situation, and refuse to go. A woman, fascinated
by his heroism and idealism, goes. That ends in their
marriage, and in the birth of a child to which they become deeply attached. Then Brand, aspiring from
height to height of devotion to his ideal, plunges from

depth to depth of murderous cruelty. First the child must die from the severity of the climate because Brand must not flinch from the post of duty and leave his congregation exposed to the peril of getting an inferior preacher in his place. Then he forces his wife to give the clothes of the dead child to a gipsy whose baby needs them. The bereaved mother does not grudge the gift; but she wants to hold back only one little garment as a relic of her darling. But Brand sees in this reservation the imperfection of the imperfect Eve. He forces her to regard the situation as a choice between the relic and his ideal. She sacrifices the relic to the ideal, and then dies, broken-hearted. Having killed her, and thereby placed himself beyond ever daring to doubt the idealism upon whose altar he has immolated her; having also refused to go to his mother's death-bed because she compromises with his principles in disposing of her property, he is hailed by the people as a saint, and finds his newly built church too small for his congregation. So he calls upon them to follow him to worship God in His own temple, the mountains. After a brief practical experience of this arrangement, they change their minds, and stone him. The very mountains themselves stone him, indeed; for he is killed by an avalanche.

PEER GYNT, 1867

Brand dies a saint, having caused more intense suffering by his saintliness than the most talented sinner could possibly have done with twice his opportunities. Ibsen does not leave this to be inferred. In another dramatic poem he gives us a rapscallion named Peer Gynt, an idealist who avoids Brand's errors by setting up as his ideal the realization of himself through the utter satisfaction of his own will. In this he would seem to be on the path to which Ibsen himself points; and indeed all who know the two plays will agree that whether or no it was better to be Peer Gynt than Brand, it was beyond all question better to be the mother or the sweetheart of Peer, scapegrace and liar as he was, than mother or wife to the saintly Brand. Brand would force his ideal on all men and women: Peer Gynt keeps his ideal for himself alone: it is indeed implicit in the ideal itself that it should be unique—that he alone should have the force to realize it. For Peer's first boyish notion of the self-realized man is not the saint, but the demigod whose indomitable will is stronger than destiny, the fighter, the master, the man whom no woman can resist, the mighty hunter, the knight of a thousand adventures, the model, in short, of the lover in a lady's novel, or the hero in a boy's romance. Now, no such person exists, or ever did exist, or ever can exist. The man who cultivates an indomitable will and refuses to make way for anything or anybody, soon finds that he cannot hold a street crossing against a tram car, much less a world against the whole human race. Only by plunging into illusions to which every fact gives the lie can he persuade himself that his will is a force that can overcome all other forces, or that it is less conditioned by circumstances than a wheelbarrow is. However, Peer Gynt, being imaginative enough to conceive his ideal, is also imaginative enough to find illusions to hide its unreality, and to persuade himself that Peer Gynt, the shabby countryside loafer, is Peer Gynt, Emperor of Himself, as he writes over the door of his hut in the mountains. His hunting feats are invented; his military genius has no solider foundation than a street fight with a smith; and his reputation as an adventurous daredevil he has to gain by the bravado of carrying off the bride from a wedding at which the guests snub him. Only in the mountains can he enjoy his illusions undisturbed by ridicule; yet even in the mountains he finds obstacles he cannot force his way through, obstacles which withstand him as spirits with voices, telling him that he must go round. But he will not: he will go forward: he will cut his path sword in hand, in spite of fate. All the same, he has to go round; for the world-will is outside Peer Gynt as well as inside him.

Then he tries the supernatural, only to find that it means nothing more than the transmogrifying of squalid realities by lies and pretences. Still, like our amateurs of thaumaturgy, he is willing to enter into a conspiracy of make-believe up to a certain point. When the Trold king's daughter appears as a repulsive ragged creature riding on a pig, he is ready to accept her as a beautiful princess on a noble steed, on condition that she accepts his mother's tumble-down farmhouse, with the broken window panes stopped up with old clouts, as a splendid castle. He will go with her among the Trolds, and pretend that the gruesome ravine in which they hold their orgies is a glorious palace; he will partake of their filthy food and declare it nectar and ambrosia; he will applaud their obscene antics as exquisite dancing, and their discordant din as divine music; but when they finally propose to slit his eyes so that he may see and hear these things, not as they are, but as he has been pretending to see and hear them, he draws back, resolved to be himself even in self-deception. He leaves the mountains and becomes a prosperous man of business in America, highly respectable and ready for any profitable speculation: slave trade, Bible trade, whisky trade, missionary trade, anything! His commercial success in this phase persuades him that he is under the special care of God; but he is shaken in his opinion by an adventure in which he is marooned on the African coast, and does not recover his faith until the treacherous friends who marooned him are destroyed before his eyes by the blowing-up of the steam yacht they have just stolen from him, when he utters his celebrated exclamation, "Ah, God is a Father to me after all; but economical he certainly is not." He finds a white horse in the desert, and is accepted on its

account as the Messiah by an Arab tribe, a success
which moves him to declare that now at last he is really
worshipped for himself, whereas in America people
only respected his breast-pin, the symbol of his money.
In commerce, too, he reflects, his eminence was a mere
matter of chance, whilst as a prophet he is eminent by
pure natural fitness for the post. This is ended by his
falling in love with a dancing-girl, who, after leading
him into every sort of undignified and ludicrous ex-
travagance, ranging from his hailing her as the Eternal-
Feminine of Goethe to the more practical folly of
giving her his white horse and all his prophetic finery,
runs away with the spoil, and leaves him once more
helpless and alone in the desert. He wanders until he
comes to the Great Sphinx, beside which he finds a
German gentleman in great perplexity as to who the
Sphinx is. Peer Gynt, seeing in that impassive, immov-
able, majestic figure, a symbol of his own ideal, is able
to tell the German gentleman at once that the Sphinx
is itself. This explanation dazzles the German, who,
after some further discussion of the philosophy of self-
realization, invites Peer Gynt to accompany him to a
club of learned men in Cairo, who are ripe for enlight-
enment on this very question. Peer, delighted, accompanies the German to the club, which turns out to be
a madhouse in which the lunatics have broken loose
and locked up their keepers. It is in this madhouse, and
by these madmen, that Peer Gynt is at last crowned
Emperor of Himself. He receives their homage as he
lies in the dust fainting with terror.

As an old man, Peer Gynt, returning to the scenes of
his early adventures, is troubled with the prospect of
meeting a certain button moulder who threatens to
make short work of his realized self by melting it
down in his crucible with a heap of other button-
material. Immediately the old exaltation of the self
realizer is changed into an unspeakable dread of the
button moulder Death, to avoid whom Peer Gynt has

already pushed a drowning man from the spar he is
clinging to in a shipwreck lest it should not suffice to
support two. At last he finds a deserted sweetheart of
his youth still waiting for him and still believing in him.
In the imagination of this old woman he finds the ideal
Peer Gynt; whilst in himself, the loafer, the braggart,
the confederate of sham magicians, the Charleston
speculator, the false prophet, the dancing-girl's dupe,
the bedlam emperor, the thruster of the drowning man
into the waves, there is nothing heroic: nothing but
commonplace self-seeking and shirking, cowardice and
sensuality, veiled only by the romantic fancies of the
born liar. With this crowningly unreal realization he is
left to face the button moulder as best he can.[1]

Peer Gynt has puzzled a good many people by
Ibsen's fantastic and subtle treatment of its metaphysi-
cal thesis. It is so far a difficult play, that the ideal of
unconditional self-realization, however familiar its sug-
gestions may be to the ambitious reader, is not understood by him. When it is stated to him by some one
who does understand it, he unhesitatingly dismisses it
as idiotic; and because he is perfectly right in doing
so—because it is idiotic in the most accurate sense of
the term—he does not easily recognize it as the com-

[1] Miss Pagan, who has produced scenes from Peer Gynt in
Edinburgh and London (which, to its shame, has not yet seen
a complete public performance of Peer Gynt), regards the death
of Peer as occurring in the scene where all the wasted possibilities of his life drift about him as withered leaves and fluffs
of bog-cotton. He picks up an onion, and, playing with the idea
that it is himself, and that its skins are the phases of his own
career wrapped round the kernel of his real self, strips them
off one after another, only to discover that there is no kernel.
"Nature is ironical," says Peer bitterly; and that discovery of his
own nothingness is taken by Miss Pagan as his death, the subsequent adventures being those of his soul. It is impossible to
demur to so poetic an interpretation; though it assumes, in spite
of the onion, that Peer had not wholly destroyed his soul. Still,
as the button moulder (who might be Brand's ghost) does
respite Peer "until the next cross roads," it cannot be said that
Ibsen leaves Peer definitely scrapped. (1912.)

mon ideal of his own prototype, the pushing, competitive, success-craving man who is the hero of the modern world.

There is nothing novel in Ibsen's dramatic method of reducing these ideals to absurdity. Exactly as Cervantes took the old ideal of chivalry, and shewed what came of a man attempting to act as if it were real, so Ibsen takes the ideals of Brand and Peer Gynt, and subjects them to the same test. Don Quixote acts as if he were a perfect knight in a world of giants and distressed damsels instead of a country gentleman in a land of innkeepers and farm wenches; Brand acts as if he were the perfect Adam in a world where, by resolute rejection of all compromise with imperfection, it was immediately possible to change the rainbow "bridge between flesh and spirit" into as enduring a structure as the tower of Babel was intended to be, thereby restoring man to the condition in which he walked with God in the garden; and Peer Gynt tries to act as if he had in him a special force that could be concentrated so as to prevail over all other forces. They ignore the real—ignore what they are and where they are, not only, like Nelson, shutting their eyes to the signals a brave man may disregard, but insanely steering straight on rocks no man's resolution can move or resist. Observe that neither Cervantes nor Ibsen is incredulous, in the Philistine way, as to the power of ideals over men. Don Quixote, Brand, and Peer Gynt are, all three, men of action seeking to realize their ideals in deeds. However ridiculous Don Quixote makes himself, you cannot dislike or despise him, much less think it would have been better for him to have been a Philistine like Sancho; and Peer Gynt, selfish rascal as he is, is not unlovable. Brand, made terrible by the consequences of his idealism to others, is heroic. Their castles in the air are more beautiful than castles of brick and mortar; but one cannot live in them; and they seduce men into pretending that every hovel is such a castle, just as **Peer Gynt** pretended that the Trold king's den was a palace.

EMPEROR AND GALILEAN, 1873

When Ibsen, by merely giving the rein to the creative impulse of his poetic nature, had produced Brand and Peer Gynt, he was nearly forty. His will, in setting his imagination to work, had produced a tough puzzle for his intellect. In no case does the difference between the will and the intellect come out more clearly than in that of the poet, save only that of the lover. Had Ibsen died in 1867, he, like many another great poet, would have gone to his grave without having ever rationally understood his own meaning. Nay, if in that year an intellectual expert—a commentator, as we call him—having read Brand, had put forward the explanation which Ibsen himself must have arrived at before he constructed Ghosts and The Wild Duck, he would perhaps have repudiated it with as much disgust as a maiden would feel if anyone were prosaic enough to give her the physiological explanation of her dreams of meeting a fairy prince. Only simpletons go to the creative artist presuming that he must be able to answer their "What does this obscure passage mean?" That is the very question the poet's own intellect, which had no part in the conception of the poem, may be asking him. And this curiosity of the intellect, this restless life in it which differentiates it from dead machinery, and troubles our lesser artists but little, is one of the marks of the greater sort. Shakespear, in Hamlet, made a drama of the self-questioning that came upon him when his intellect rose up in alarm, as well it might, against the vulgar optimism of his Henry V, and yet could mend it to no better purpose than by the equally vulgar pessimism of Troilus and Cressida. Dante took

pains to understand himself: so did Goethe. Richard
Wagner, one of the greatest poets of our own day, has
left us as many volumes of criticism of art and life as
he has left musical scores; and he has expressly described how the keen intellectual activity he brought
to the analysis of his music dramas was in abeyance
during their creation. Just so do we find Ibsen, after
composing his two great dramatic poems, entering on a
struggle to become intellectually conscious of what he
had done.

We have seen that with Shakespear such an effort
became itself creative and produced a drama of ques-
tioning. With Ibsen the same thing occurred: he harked
back to an abandoned project of his, and wrote two
huge dramas on the subject of the apostasy of the Emperor Julian. In this work we find him at first preoccu-
pied with a piece of old-fashioned freethinking: the
dilemma that moral responsibility presupposes free-will,
and that free-will sets man above God. Cain, who slew
because he willed, willed because he must, and must
have willed to slay because he was himself, comes upon
the stage to claim that murder is fertile, and death the
ground of life, though, not having read Weismann on
death as a method of evolution, he cannot say what
is the ground of death. Judas asks whether, when the
Master chose him, he chose foreknowingly. This part
of the drama has no very deep significance. It is easy
to invent conundrums which dogmatic evangelicalism
cannot answer; and no doubt, whilst it was still a nine
days' wonder that evangelicalism could not solve all
enigmas, such invention seemed something much deeper
than the mere intellectual chess-play which it is seen
to be now that the nine days are past. In his occasional
weakness for such conundrums, and later on in his
harping on the hereditary transmission of disease, we
see Ibsen's active intellect busy, not only with the
problems peculiar to his own plays, but with the fatalism and pessimism of the middle of the nineteenth

century, when the typical advanced culture was attainable by reading Strauss's Leben Jesu, the popularizations of Helmholtz and Darwin by Tyndall and Huxley, and George Eliot's novels, vainly protested against by Ruskin as peopled with "the sweepings of a Pentonville omnibus." The traces of this period in Ibsen's writings shew how well he knew the crushing weight with which the sordid cares of the ordinary struggle for money and respectability fell on the world when the romance of the creeds was discredited, and progress seemed for the moment to mean, not the growth of the spirit of man, but an effect of the survival of the fittest brought about by the destruction of the unfit, all the most frightful examples of this systematic destruction being thrust into the utmost prominence by those who were fighting the Church with Mill's favorite dialectical weapon, the incompatibility of divine omnipotence with divine benevolence. His plays are full of an overwhelming sense of the necessity for rousing ourselves into self-assertion against this numbing fatalism; and yet he certainly had not at this time freed his intellect from an acceptance of its scientific validity as our Samuel Butler did, though Butler was more like Ibsen than any man in Europe, having the same grim hoaxing humor, the same grip of spiritual realities behind material facts, the same toughness of character holding him unshaken against the world.

Butler revelled in Darwinism for six weeks, and then, grasping the whole scope and the whole horror of it, warned us (we did not listen until we had revelled for half a century) that Darwin had "banished mind from the universe," meaning from Evolution. Ibsen, belonging to an earlier generation, and intellectually nursed on northern romance and mysticism rather than on the merely industrious and prosaic science of the interval between the discovery of Evolution at the end of the eighteenth century and the discovery and overrating of Natural Selection as a method of evolution in the middle of the nineteenth, was, when Darwin arrived, past the age at which Natural Selection could have swept him away as it swept Butler and his contemporaries. But, like them, he seems to have welcomed it for the mortal blow it dealt to the current travesties of Christianity, which were really only reductions of the relations between man and God to the basis of the prevalent Commercialism, shewing how God may be cheated, and how salvation can be got for nothing through the blood of Christ by sweaters, adulterators, quacks, sharks, and hypocrites; also how God, though the most dangerously capricious and short-tempered of Anarchists, is also the most sentimental of dupes. It is against this conception of God as a sentimental dupe that Brand rages. Ibsen evidently regarded the brimstone conception, "the Almighty Fiend" of Shelley, as not worth his powder and shot, partly, no doubt, because he knew that the Almighty Fiend's votaries would never read or understand his works, and partly because the class he addressed, the cultured class, had thrown off that superstition, and were busy with the sentimental religion of love in which we are still wallowing, and which only substitutes twaddle for terror.

At first sight this may seem an improvement; but it is no defence against that fear of man which is so much more mischievous than the fear of God. The cruelty of Natural Selection was a powerful antidote to such sentimentalism; and Ibsen, who was perhaps no expert in recent theories of evolution, was quite ready to rub it in uncritically for the sake of its value as a tonic. Indeed, as a fearless observer of the cruelty of Nature, he was quite independent of Darwin: what we find in his works is an unmistakable Darwinian atmosphere, but not the actual Darwinian discoveries and technical theory. If Natural Selection, the gloomiest and most formidable of the castles of Giant Despair, had stopped him, he would no doubt, like Butler, have set himself deliberately to play Greatheart and reduce it; but his genius pushed him past it and left it to be demolished philosophically by Butler, and practically by the mere march of the working class, which, by its freedom from the economic bias of the middle classes, has escaped their characteristic illusions, and solved many of the enigmas they found insoluble because they did not wish to have them solved. For instance, according to the theory of Natural Selection, progress can take place only through an increase in the severity of the material conditions of existence; and as the working classes were quite determined that progress should consist of just the opposite, they had no difficulty in seeing that it generally does occur in that way, whereas the middle class wished, on the contrary, to be convinced that the poverty of the working classes and all the hideous evils attending it were inevitable conditions of progress, and that every penny in the pound on the rates spent in social amelioration, and every attempt on the part of the workers to raise their wages by Trade Unionism or otherwise, were vain defiances of biologic and economic science.

How far Ibsen was definitely conscious of all this is doubtful; but one of his most famous utterances pointed to the working class and the women as the great emancipators. His prophetic belief in the spontaneous growth of the will made him a meliorist without reference to the operation of Natural Selection; but his impression of the light thrown by physical and biological science on the facts of life seems to have been the gloomy one of the middle of the nineteenth century. External nature often plays her most ruthless and destructive part in his works, which have an extraordinary fascination for the pessimists of that period, in spite of the incompatibility of his individualism with that mechanical utilitarian ethic of theirs which treats Man as the sport of every circumstance, and ignores his will altogether.

Another inessential but very prominent feature in Ibsen's dramas will be understood easily by anyone who has observed how a change of religious faith intensifies our concern about our own salvation. An ideal, pious or secular, is practically used as a standard of conduct; and whilst it remains unquestioned, the simple rule of right is to conform to it. In the theological stage, when the Bible is accepted as the revelation of God's will, the pious man, when in doubt as to whether he is acting rightly or wrongly, quiets his misgivings by searching the Scripture until he finds a text which endorses his action.[1] The rationalist, for whom the Bible has no authority, brings his conduct to such tests as asking himself, after Kant, how it would be if everyone did as he proposes to do; or by calculating the effect of his action on the greatest happiness of the greatest number; or by judging whether the liberty of action he is claiming infringes the equal liberty of others, etc. etc. Most men are ingenious enough to pass examinations of this kind successfully in respect to everything they really want to do. But in periods of transition, as, for instance, when faith in the infallibility of the Bible is shattered, and faith in that of reason not yet perfected, men's uncertainty as to the rightness and wrongness of their actions keeps them in a continual perplexity, amid which casuistry seems the most important branch of intellectual activity. Life, as depicted by Ibsen, is very full of it. We find the great double drama of Emperor and Galilean occupied at first with Julian's case regarded as a case of conscience. It is compared, in the manner already described, with the cases of Cain and Judas, the three men being introduced as "corner stones under the wrath of necessity," "great freedmen under necessity," and so forth. The qualms of Julian are theatrically effective in producing the most exciting suspense as to whether he will dare to choose between

---

[1] As such misgivings seldom arise except when the conscience revolts against the contemplated action, an appeal to Scripture to justify a point of conduct is generally found in practice to be an attempt to excuse a crime.

Christ and the imperial purple; but the mere exhibition of a man struggling between his ambition and his creed belongs to a phase of intellectual interest which Ibsen had passed even before the production of Brand, when he wrote his Kongs Emnerne (The Pretenders). Emperor and Galilean might have been appropriately, if prosaically, named The Mistake of Maximus the Mystic. It is Maximus who forces the choice on Julian, not as between ambition and principle; between Paganism and Christianity; between "the old beauty that is no longer beautiful and the new truth that is no longer true," but between Christ and Julian himself. Maximus knows that there is no going back to "the first empire" of pagan sensualism. "The second empire," Christian or self-abnegatory idealism, is already rotten at heart. "The third empire" is what he looks for: the empire of Man asserting the eternal validity of his own will. He who can see that not on Olympus, not nailed to the cross, but in himself is God: he is the man to build, Brand's bridge between the flesh and the spirit, establishing this third empire in which the spirit shall not be unknown, nor the flesh starved, nor the will tortured and baffled. Thus throughout the first part of the double drama we have Julian prompted step by step to the stupendous conviction that he no less than the Galilean is God. His final resolution to seize the throne is expressed in his interruption of the Lord's prayer, which he hears intoned by worshippers in church as he wrestles in the gloom of the catacombs with his own fears and the entreaties and threats of his soldiers urging him to take the final decisive step. At the cue "Lead us not into temptation; but deliver us from evil" he rushes to the church with his soldiers, exclaiming "For mine is the kingdom." Yet he halts on the threshold, dazzled by the light, as his follower Sallust points the declaration by adding, "and the power, and the glory."

Once on the throne Julian becomes a mere pedant-tyrant, trying to revive Paganism mechanically by cruel enforcement of external conformity to its rites. In his moments of exaltation he half grasps the meaning of Maximus, only to relapse presently and pervert it into a grotesque mixture of superstition and monstrous vanity. We have him making such speeches as this, worthy of Peer Gynt at his most ludicrous: "Has not Plato long ago enunciated the truth that only a god can rule over men? What did he mean by that saying? Answer me: what did he mean? Far be it from me to assert that Plato, incomparable sage though he was, had any individual, even the greatest, in his prophetic eye," etc. In this frame of mind Christ appears to him, not as the prototype of himself, as Maximus would have him feel, but as a rival god over whom he must prevail at all costs. It galls him to think that the Galilean still reigns in the hearts of men whilst the emperor can only extort lip honor from them by brute force; for in his wildest excesses of egotism he never so loses his saving sense of the realities of things as to mistake the trophies of persecution for the fruits of faith. "Tell me who shall conquer," he demands of Maximus: "the emperor or the Galilean?"

"Both the emperor and the Galilean shall succumb," says Maximus. "Whether in our time or in hundreds of years I know not; but so it shall be when the right man comes."

"Who is the right man?" says Julian.

"He who shall swallow up both emperor and Galilean," [2] replies the seer. "Both shall succumb; but you shall not therefore perish. Does not the child succumb in the youth and the youth in the man: yet neither child nor youth perishes. You know I have never approved of your policy as emperor. You have tried to make the youth a child again. The empire of the flesh is fallen a prey to the empire of the spirit. But the empire of the spirit is not final, any more than the youth is. You have tried to hinder the youth from

[2] Or, as we should now say, the Superman. (1912.)

growing: from becoming a man. Oh fool, who have
drawn your sword against that which is to be: against
the third empire, in which the twin-natured shall reign.
For him the Jews have a name. They call him Messiah,
and are waiting for him."

Still Julian stumbles on the threshold of the idea
without entering into it. He is galled out of all com-
prehension by the rivalry of the Galilean, and asks
despairingly who shall break his power. Then Maximus
drives the lesson home.

MAXIMUS. Is it not written, "Thou shalt have none
other gods but me?"

JULIAN. Yes—yes—yes.

MAXIMUS. The seer of Nazareth did not preach this
god or that: he said "God is I: I am God."

JULIAN. And that is what makes the emperor power-
less? The third empire? The Messiah? Not the Jews'
Messiah, but the Messiah of the two empires, the spirit
and the world?

MAXIMUS. The God-Emperor.

JULIAN. The Emperor-God.

MAXIMUS. Logos in Pan, Pan in Logos.

JULIAN. How is he begotten?

MAXIMUS. He is self-begotten in the man who wills.

But it is of no use. Maximus's idea is a synthesis of
relations in which not only is Christ God in exactly the
same sense as that in which Julian is God, but Julian is
Christ as well. The persistence of Julian's jealousy of
the Galilean shews that he has not comprehended the
synthesis at all, but only seized on that part of it which
flatters his own egotism. And since this part is only
valid as a constituent of the synthesis, and has no reality
when isolated from it, it cannot by itself convince
Julian. In vain does Maximus repeat his lesson in every
sort of parable, and in such pregnant questions as "How
do you know, Julian, that you were not in him whom
you now persecute?" He can only wreak him to utter
commands to the winds, and to exclaim, in the excite-

ment of burning his fleet on the borders of Persia, "The third empire is here, Maximus. I feel that the Messiah of the earth lives within me. The spirit has become flesh and the flesh spirit. All creation lies within my will and power. More than the fleet is burning. In that glowing, swirling pyre the crucified Galilean is burning to ashes; and the earthly emperor is burning with the Galilean. But from the ashes shall arise, phœnix-like, the God of earth and the Emperor of the spirit in one, in one, in one." At which point he is informed that a Persian refugee, whose information has emboldened him to burn his ships, has fled from the camp and is a manifest spy. From that moment he is a broken man. In his next and last emergency, when the Persians fall upon his camp, his first desperate exclamation is a vow to sacrifice to the gods. "To what gods, oh fool?" cries Maximus. "Where are they; and what are they?" "I will sacrifice to this god and that god: I will sacrifice to many," he answers desperately. "One or other must surely hear me. *I must call on something without me and above me.*" A flash of lightning seems to him a response from above; and with this encouragement he throws himself into the fight, clinging, like Macbeth, to an ambiguous oracle which leads him to suppose that only in the Phrygian regions need he fear defeat. He imagines he sees the Nazarene in the ranks of the enemy; and in fighting madly to reach him he is struck down, in the name of Christ, by one of his own soldiers. Then his one Christian General, Jovian, calls on his "believing brethren" to give Cæsar what is Cæsar's. Declaring that the heavens are open and the angels coming to the rescue with their swords of fire, he rallies the Galileans of whom Julian has made slave-soldiers. The pagan free legions, crying out that the god of the Galileans is on the Roman side, and that he is the strongest, follow Jovian as he charges the enemy, who fly in all directions whilst Julian, sinking back

from a vain effort to rise, exclaims, "Thou hast conquered, O Galilean."

Julian dies quietly in his tent, averring, in reply to
a Christian friend's inquiry, that he has nothing to re-
pent of. "The power which circumstances placed in
my hands," he says, "and which is an emanation of
divinity, I am conscious of having used to the best of
my skill. I have never wittingly wronged anyone. If
some should think that I have not fulfilled all expecta-
tions, they should in justice reflect that there is a mys-
terious power outside us, which in a great measure
governs the issue of human undertakings." He still does
not see eye to eye with Maximus, though there is a
flash of insight in his remark to him, when he learns
that the village where he fell is called the Phrygian
region, that "the world-will has laid an ambush for
him." It was something for Julian to have seen that the
power which he found stronger than his individual will
was itself will; but inasmuch as he conceived it, not as
the whole of which his will was but a part, but as a
rival will, he was not the man to found the third empire. He had felt the godhead in himself, but not in
others. Being only able to say, with half conviction,
"The kingdom of heaven is within ME," he had been
utterly vanquished by the Galilean who had been able
to say, "The kingdom of heaven is within YOU." But
he was on the way to that full truth. A man cannot
believe in others until he believes in himself; for his
conviction of the equal worth of his fellows must be
filled by the overflow of his conviction of his own
worth. Against the spurious Christianity of asceticism,
starving that indispensable prior conviction, Julian
rightly rebelled: and Maximus rightly incited him to
rebel. But Maximus could not fill the prior conviction
even to fulness, much less to overflowing; for the third
empire was not yet, and is not yet.

However, the tyrant dies with a peaceful conscience;
and Maximus is able to tell the priest at the bedside that

the world-will will answer for Julian's soul. What troubles the mystic is his having misled Julian by encouraging him to bring upon himself the fate of Cain and Judas. As water can be boiled by fire, man can be prompted and stimulated from without to assert his individuality; but just as no boiling can fill a half-empty well, no external stimulus can enlarge the spirit of man to the point at which he can self-beget the Emperor-God in himself by willing. At that point "to will is to have to will"; and it is with these words on his lips that Maximus leaves the stage, still sure that the third empire is to come.

It is not necessary to translate the scheme of Emperor and Galilean into terms of the antithesis between idealism and realism. Julian, in this respect, is a reincarnation of Peer Gynt. All the difference is that the subject which was instinctively projected in the earlier poem, is intellectually constructed in the later history, Julian plus Maximus the Mystic being Peer plus one who understands him better than Ibsen did when he created him.

The interest for us of Ibsen's interpretation of original Christianity is obvious. The deepest sayings recorded in the gospels are now nothing but eccentric paradoxes to most of those who reject the supernatural view of Christ's divinity. Those who accept that view often consider that such acceptance absolves them from attaching any sensible meaning to his words at all, and so might as well pin their faith to a stock or stone. Of these attitudes the first is superficial, and the second stupid. Ibsen's interpretation, whatever my be its validity, will certainly hold the field long after the current "Crosstianity," as it has been aptly called, becomes unthinkable.

THE OBJECTIVE ANTI-IDEALIST
PLAYS

IBSEN had now written three immense dramas, all dealing with the effect of idealism on individual egotists of exceptional imaginative excitability. This he was able to do whilst his intellectual consciousness of his theme was yet incomplete, by simply portraying sides of himself. He has put himself into the skin of Brand and Peer Gynt. He has divided himself between Maximus and Julian. These figures have accordingly a certain direct vitality which we shall find in none of his later male figures until it reappears under the shadow of death, less as vitality than as mortality putting on immortality, in the four great plays with which he closed and crowned his life's work. There are flashes of it in Relling, in Lövborg, in Ellida's stranger from the sea; but they are only flashes: henceforth for many years, indeed until his warfare against vulgar idealism is accomplished and a new phase entered upon in The Master Builder, all his really vivid and solar figures are women. For, having at last completed his intellectual analysis of idealism, he could now construct methodical illustrations of its social working, instead of, as before, blindly projecting imaginary personal experiences which he himself had not yet succeeded in interpreting. Further, now that he understood the matter, he could see plainly the effect of idealism as a social force on people quite unlike himself: that is to say, on everyday people in everyday life: on shipbuilders, bank managers, parsons, and doctors, as well as on saints, romantic adventurers, and emperors.

With his eyes thus opened, instances of the mischief of idealism crowded upon him so rapidly that he began deliberately to inculcate their lesson by writing realistic prose plays of modern life, abandoning all production of art for art's sake. His skill as a playwright and his genius as an artist were thenceforth used only to secure attention and effectiveness for his detailed attack on idealism. No more verse, no more tragedy for the sake of tears or comedy for the sake of laughter, no more seeking to produce specimens of art forms in order that literary critics might fill the public belly with the east wind. The critics, it is true, soon declared that he had ceased to be an artist; but he, having something else to do with his talent than to fulfil critics' definitions, took no notice of them, not thinking their ideal sufficiently important to write a play about.

THE LEAGUE OF YOUTH, 1869

The first of the series of realistic prose plays is called Pillars of Society; but before describing this, a word must be said about a previous work which seems to have determined the form the later series took. Between Peer Gynt and Emperor and Galilean, Ibsen had let fall an amusing comedy called The League of Youth (*De Unges Forbund*) in which the imaginative egotist reappears farcically as an ambitious young lawyer-politician who, smarting under a snub from a local landowner and county magnate, relieves his feelings with such a passionate explosion of Radical eloquence that he is cheered to the echo by the progressive party.

Intoxicated with this success, he imagines himself a great leader of the people and a wielder of the mighty engine of democracy. He narrates to a friend a dream in which he saw kings swept helplessly over the surface of the earth by a mighty wind. He has hardly achieved this impromptu when he receives an invitation to dine with the local magnate, whose friends, to spare his feelings, have misled him as to the person aimed at in the new demagogue's speech. The invitation sets the egotist's imagination on the opposite tack: he is presently pouring forth his soul in the magnate's drawing-room to the very friend to whom he related the great dream.

"My goal is this: in the course of time I shall get into Parliament, perhaps into the Ministry, and marry happily into a rich and honorable family. I intend to reach it by my own exertions. I must and shall reach it without help from anyone. Meanwhile I shall enjoy life here, drinking in beauty and sunshine. Here there are fine manners: life moves gracefully here: the very floors seem laid to be trodden only by lacquered shoes: the arm-chairs are deep; and the ladies sink exquisitely into them. Here the conversation goes lightly and elegantly, like a game at battledore; and no blunders come plumping in to make an awkward silence. Here I feel for the first time what distinction means. Yes: we have indeed an aristocracy of culture; and to it I will belong. Dont you yourself feel the refining influence of the place," etc., etc.

For the rest, the play is an ingenious comedy of intrigue, clever enough in its mechanical construction to entitle the French to claim that Ibsen owes something to his technical education as a playwright in the school of Scribe. One or two episodes are germs of later plays; and the suitability of the realistic prose comedy form to these episodes no doubt confirmed Ibsen in his choice of it.

PILLARS OF SOCIETY, 1877

Pillars of Society is the history of one Karsten Bernick, a "pillar of society" who, in pursuance of the duty of maintaining the respectability of his father's firm of shipbuilders, has averted a disgraceful exposure by allowing another man to bear the discredit not only of a love affair in which he himself had been the sinner, but of a theft which was never committed at all, having been merely alleged as an excuse for the firm being out of funds at a critical period. Bernick is an abject slave to the idealizings of one Rörlund, a schoolmaster, about respectability, duty to society, good example, social influence, health of the community, and so on. When Bernick falls in love with a married actress, he feels that no man has a right to shock the feelings of Rörlund and the community for his own selfish gratification. However, a clandestine intrigue will shock nobody, since nobody need know of it. He accordingly adopts this method of satisfying himself and preserving the moral tone of the community at the same time. Unluckily, the intrigue is all but discovered; and Bernick has either to see the moral security of the community shaken to its foundations by the terrible scandal of his exposure, or else to deny what he did and put it on another man. As the other man happens to be going to America, where he can easily conceal his imputed shame, Bernick's conscience tells him that it would be little short of a crime against society to neglect such an opportunity; and he accordingly lies his way back into the good opinion of Rörlund and Company at the emigrant's expense.

There are three women in the play for whom the schoolmaster's ideals have no attractions. First, there is the actress's daughter, who wants to get to America because she hears that people there are not good; for

she is heartily tired of good people, since it is part of
their goodness to look down on her because of her
mother's disgrace. The schoolmaster, to whom she is
engaged, condescends to her for the same reason. The
second has already sacrificed her happiness and wasted
her life in conforming to the Rörlund ideal of womanliness; and she earnestly advises the younger woman not
to commit that folly, but to break her engagement
with the schoolmaster, and elope promptly with the
man she loves. The third is a naturally free woman who
has snapped her fingers at the current ideals all her
life; and it is her presence that at last encourages the
liar to break with the ideals by publicly telling the
truth about himself.

The comic personage of the piece is a useless hypo-
chondriac whose function in life, as described by himself, is "to hold up the banner of the ideal." This he
does by sneering at everything and everybody for not
resembling the heroic incidents and characters he reads
about in novels and tales of adventure. But his obvious
peevishness and folly make him much less dangerous
than the pious idealist, the earnest and respectable Rörlund. The play concludes with Bernick's admission
that the spirits of Truth and Freedom are the true
pillars of society, a phrase which sounds so like an
idealistic commonplace that it is necessary to add that
Truth in this passage does not mean the nursery convention of truth-telling satirized by Ibsen himself in a
later play, as well as by Labiche and other comic drama-
tists. It means the unflinching recognition of facts, and
the abandonment of the conspiracy to ignore such of
them as do not bolster up the ideals. The idealist rule
as to truth dictates the recognition only of those facts
or idealistic masks of facts which have a respectable air,
and the mentioning of these on all occasions and at all
hazards. Ibsen urges the recognition of all facts; but as
to mentioning them, he wrote a whole play, as we shall
see presently, to shew that you must do that at your

own peril, and that a truth-teller who cannot hold his tongue on occasion may do as much mischief as a whole universityful of trained liars. The word Freedom means freedom from the tyranny of the Rörlund ideals.

A DOLL'S HOUSE, 1879

Unfortunately, Pillars of Society, as a propagandist play, is disabled by the circumstance that the hero, being a fraudulent hypocrite in the ordinary police-court sense of the phrase, would hardly be accepted as a typical pillar of society by the class he represents. Accordingly, Ibsen took care next time to make his idealist irreproachable from the standpoint of the ordinary idealist morality. In the famous Doll's House, the pillar of society who owns the doll is a model husband, father, and citizen. In his little household, with the three darling children and the affectionate little wife, all on the most loving terms with one another, we have the sweet home, the womanly woman, the happy family life of the idealist's dream. Mrs. Nora Helmer is happy in the belief that she has attained a valid realization of all these illusions; that she is an ideal wife and mother; and that Helmer is an ideal husband who would, if the necessity arose, give his life to save her reputation. A few simply contrived incidents disabuse her effectually on all these points. One of her earliest acts of devotion to her husband has been the secret raising of a sum of money to enable him to make a tour which was necessary to restore his health. As he would have broken down sooner than go into debt, she has had to persuade him that the money was a gift from her father. It was really obtained from a moneylender, who refused to make her the loan unless she induced her father to endorse the promissory note. This being impossible, as her father was dying at the time, she took the shortest way out of the difficulty by writing the name herself, to the entire satisfaction of the moneylender, who, though not at all duped, knew that forged bills are often the surest to be paid. Since then she has slaved in secret at scrivener's work until she has nearly paid off the debt.

At this point Helmer is made manager of the bank in which he is employed; and the moneylender, wishing to obtain a post there, uses the forged bill to force Nora to exert her influence with Helmer on his behalf. But she, having a hearty contempt for the man, cannot be persuaded by him that there was any harm in putting her father's name on the bill, and ridicules the suggestion that the law would not recognize that she was right under the circumstances. It is her husband's own contemptuous denunciation of a forgery formerly committed by the moneylender himself that destroys her self-satisfaction and opens her eyes to her ignorance of the serious business of the world to which her husband belongs: the world outside the home he shares with her. When he goes on to tell her that commercial dishonesty is generally to be traced to the influence of bad mothers, she begins to perceive that the happy way in which she plays with the children, and the care she takes to dress them nicely, are not sufficient to constitute her a fit person to train them. To redeem the forged bill, she resolves to borrow the balance due upon it from an intimate friend of the family. She has learnt to coax her husband into giving her what she asks by appealing to his affection for her: that is, by playing all sorts of pretty tricks until he is wheedled into an amorous humor. This plan she has adopted without thinking about it, instinctively taking the line of least resistance with him. And now she naturally takes the same line with her husband's friend. An unexpected declaration of love from him is the result; and it at once explains to her the real nature of the domestic influence she has been so proud of.

All her illusions about herself are now shattered.

She sees herself as an ignorant and silly woman, a dangerous mother, and a wife kept for her husband's pleasure merely; but she clings all the harder to her illusion about him: he is still the ideal husband who would make any sacrifice to rescue her from ruin. She resolves to kill herself rather than allow him to destroy his own career by taking the forgery on himself to save her reputation. The final disillusion comes when he, instead of at once proposing to pursue this ideal line of conduct when he hears of the forgery, naturally enough flies into a vulgar rage and heaps invective on her for disgracing him. Then she sees that their whole family life has been a fiction: their home a mere doll's house in which they have been playing at ideal husband and father, wife and mother. So she leaves him then and there and goes out into the real world to find out its reality for herself, and to gain some position not fundamentally false, refusing to see her children again until she is fit to be in charge of them, or to live with him until she and he become capable of a more honorable relation to one another. He at first cannot understand what has happened, and flourishes the shattered ideals over her as if they were as potent as ever. He presents the course most agreeable to him—that of her staying at home and avoiding a scandal—as her duty to her husband, to her children, and to her religion; but the magic of these disguises is gone; and at last even he understands what has really happened, and sits down alone to wonder whether that more honorable relation can ever come to pass between them.

GHOSTS, 1881

In his next play, Ibsen returned to the charge with such an uncompromising and outspoken attack on marriage as a useless sacrifice of human beings to an ideal, that his meaning was obscured by its very obviousness. Ghosts, as it is called, is the story of a woman who has faithfully acted as a model wife and mother, sacrificing herself at every point with selfless thoroughness. Her husband is a man with a huge capacity and appetite for sensuous enjoyment. Society, prescribing ideal duties and not enjoyment for him, drives him to enjoy himself in underhand and illicit ways. When he marries his model wife, her devotion to duty only makes life harder for him; and he at last takes refuge in the caresses of an undutiful but pleasure-loving housemaid, and leaves his wife to satisfy her conscience by managing his business affairs whilst he satisfies his cravings as best he can by reading novels, drinking, and flirting, as aforesaid, with the servants. At this point even those who are most indignant with Nora Helmer for walking out of the doll's house must admit that Mrs. Alving would be justified in walking out of *her* house. But Ibsen is determined to shew you what comes of the scrupulous line of conduct you were so angry with Nora for not pursuing. Mrs. Alving feels that her place is by her husband for better for worse, and by her child. Now the ideal of wifely and womanly duty which demands this from her also demands that she shall regard herself as an outraged wife, and her husband as a scoundrel. And the family ideal calls upon her to suffer in silence lest she shatter her innocent son's faith in the purity of home life by letting him know the disreputable truth about his father. It is her duty to conceal that truth from the world and from him. In this she falters for one moment only. Her marriage has not been a love match: she has, in pursuance of her duty as a daughter, contracted it for the sake of her family, although her heart inclined to a highly respectable clergyman, a professor of her own idealism, named Manders. In the humiliation of her first discovery of her husband's infidelity, she leaves the house and takes refuge with Manders;

but he at once leads her back to the path of duty, from which she does not again swerve. With the utmost devotion she now carries out an elaborate scheme of lying and imposture. She so manages her husband's affairs and so shields his good name that everybody believes him to be a public-spirited citizen of the strictest conformity to current ideals of respectability and family life. She sits up of nights listening to his lewd and silly conversation, and even drinking with him, to keep him from going into the streets and being detected by the neighbors in what she considers his vices. She provides for the servant he has seduced, and brings up his illegitimate daughter as a maid in her own household. And, as a crowning sacrifice, she sends her son away to Paris to be educated there, knowing that if he stays at home the shattering of his ideals must come sooner or later.

Her work is crowned with success. She gains the esteem of her old love the clergyman, who is never tired of holding up her household as a beautiful realization of the Christian ideal of marriage. Her own martyrdom is brought to an end at last by the death of her husband in the odor of a most sanctified reputation, leaving her free to recall her son from Paris and enjoy his society, and his love and gratitude, in the flower of his early manhood.

But when her son comes home, the facts refuse as obstinately as ever to correspond to her ideals. Oswald has inherited his father's love of enjoyment; and when, in dull rainy weather, he returns from Paris to the solemn strictly ordered house where virtue and duty have had their temple for so many years, his mother sees him shew the unmistakable signs of boredom with which she is so miserably familiar from of old; then sit after dinner killing time over the bottle; and finally —the climax of anguish—begin to flirt with the maid who, as his mother alone knows, is his own father's daughter. But there is this worldwide difference in her insight to the cases of the father and the son. She did not love the father: she loves the son with the intensity of a heart-starved woman who has nothing else left to love. Instead of recoiling from him with pious disgust and Pharisaical consciousness of moral superiority, she sees at once that he has a right to be happy in his own way, and that she has no right to force him to be dutiful and wretched in hers. She sees, too, her injustice to the unfortunate father, and the cowardice of the monstrous fabric of lies and false appearances she has wasted her life in manufacturing. She resolves that the son's life shall not be sacrificed to ideals which are to him joyless and unnatural. But she finds that the work of the ideals is not to be un-done quite so easily. In driving the father to steal his pleasures in secrecy and squalor, they had brought upon him the diseases bred by such conditions; and her son now tells her that those diseases have left their mark on him, and that he carries poison in his pocket against the time, foretold to him by a Parisian surgeon, when general paralysis of the insane may destroy his faculties. In desperation she undertakes to rescue him from this horrible apprehension by making his life happy. The house shall be made as bright as Paris for him: he shall have as much champagne as he wishes until he is no longer driven to that dangerous resource by the dulness of his life with her: if he loves the girl he shall marry her if she were fifty times his half-sister. But the half-sister, on learning the state of his health, leaves the house; for she, too, is her father's daughter, and is not going to sacrifice her life in devotion to an invalid. When the mother and son are left alone in their dreary home, with the rain still falling outside, all she can do for him is to promise that if his doom overtakes him before he can poison himself, she will make a final sacrifice of her natural feelings by per-forming that dreadful duty, the first of all her duties that has any real basis. Then the weather clears up at last; and the sun, which the young man has so longed to see, appears. He asks her to give it to him to play with; and a glance at him shews her that the ideals have claimed their victim, and that the time has come for her to save him from a real horror by sending him from her out of the world, just as she saved him from an imaginary one years before by sending him out of Norway.

The last scene of Ghosts is so appallingly tragic that the emotions it excites prevent the meaning of the play from being seized and discussed like that of A Doll's House. In England nobody, as far as I know, seems to have perceived that Ghosts is to A Doll's House what the late Sir Walter Besant intended his own sequel [1] to that play to be. Besant attempted to shew what might come of Nora's repudiation of that idealism of which he was one of the most popular professors. But the effect made on Besant by A Doll's House was very faint compared to that produced on the English critics by the first performance of Ghosts in this country. In the earlier part of this essay I have shewn that since Mrs. Alving's early conceptions of duty are as valid to ordinary critics as to Pastor Man-

---

[1] A forgotten production, published in the English Illustrated Magazine for January 1890. Besant makes the moneylender, as a reformed man, and a pattern of all the virtues, hold a forged bill *in terrorem* over Nora's grown-up daughter, engaged to his son. The bill has been forged by her brother, who has inherited a tendency to forge from his mother. Helmer having taken to drink after the departure of his wife, and forfeited his social position, the moneylender tells the girl that if she persists in disgracing him by marrying his son, he will send her brother to gaol. She evades the dilemma by drowning herself. The moral is that if Nora had never run away from her husband her daughter would never have drowned herself. Note that the moneylender does over again what he did in Ibsen's play, with the difference that, having become eminently respectable, he has also become a remorseless scoundrel. Ibsen shews him as a good-natured fellow at bottom. I wrote a sequel to this sequel. Another sequel was written by Eleanor, the youngest daughter of Karl Marx. I forget where they appeared.

ders, who must appear to them as an admirable man, endowed with Helmer's good sense without Helmer's selfishness, a pretty general disapproval of the moral of the play was inevitable. Fortunately, the newspaper press went to such bedlamite lengths on this occasion that Mr. William Archer, the well-known dramatic critic and translator of Ibsen, was able to put the whole body of hostile criticism out of court by simply quoting its excesses in an article entitled Ghosts and Gibberings, which appeared in The Pall Mall Gazette of the 8th of April 1891. Mr. Archer's extracts, which he offers as a nucleus for a Dictionary of Abuse modelled upon the Wagner *Schimpf-Lexicon*, are worth reprinting here as samples of contemporary idealist criticism of the drama.

DESCRIPTIONS OF THE PLAY

"Ibsen's positively abominable play entitled Ghosts . . . This disgusting representation . . . Reprobation due to such as aim at infecting the modern theatre with poison after desperately inoculating themselves and others . . . An open drain; a loathsome sore unbandaged; a dirty act done publicly; a lazar-house with all its doors and windows open . . . Candid foulness . . . Kotzebue turned bestial and cynical. Offensive cynicism . . . Ibsen's melancholy and malodorous world . . . Absolutely loathsome and fetid . . . Gross, almost putrid indecorum . . . Literary carrion . . . Crapulous stuff . . . Novel and perilous nuisance." *Daily Telegraph* [leading article]. "This mass of vulgarity, egotism, coarseness, and absurdity." *Daily Telegraph* [criticism]. "Unutterably offensive . . . Prosecution under Lord Campbell's Act . . . Abominable piece . . . Scandalous." *Standard.* "Naked loathsomeness . . . Most dismal and repulsive production." *Daily News.* "Revoltingly suggestive and blasphemous

. . . Characters either contradictory in themselves, un-interesting or abhorrent." *Daily Chronicle.* "A re-pulsive and degrading work." *Queen.* "Morbid, un-healthy, unwholesome and disgusting story . . . A piece to bring the stage into disrepute and dishonour with every right-thinking man and woman." *Lloyd's.* "Merely dull dirt long drawn out." *Hawk.* "Morbid horrors of the hideous tale . . . Ponderous dulness of the didactic talk . . . If any repetition of this outrage be attempted, the authorities will doubtless wake from their lethargy." *Sporting and Dramatic News.* "Just a wicked nightmare." *The Gentlewoman.* "Lugubrious diagnosis of sordid impropriety . . . Characters are prigs, pedants, and profligates . . . Morbid caricatures . . . Maunderings of nookshotten Norwegians . . . It is no more of a play than an average Gaiety bur-lesque." *Black and White.* "Most loathsome of all Ibsen's plays . . . Garbage and offal." *Truth.* "Ibsen's putrid play called Ghosts . . . So loathsome an enter-prise." *Academy.* "As foul and filthy a concoction as has ever been allowed to disgrace the boards of an English theatre . . . Dull and disgusting . . . Nasti-ness and malodorousness laid on thickly as with a trowel." *Era.* "Noisome corruption." *Stage.*

DESCRIPTIONS OF IBSEN

"An egotist and a bungler." *Daily Telegraph.* "A crazy fanatic . . . A crazy, cranky being . . . Not only consistently dirty but deplorably dull." *Truth.* "The Norwegian pessimist *in petto*" [*sic*]. *Black and White.* "Ugly, nasty, discordant, and downright dull . . . A gloomy sort of ghoul, bent on groping for horrors by night, and blinking like a stupid old owl when the warm sunlight of the best of life dances into his wrinkled eyes." *Gentlewoman.* "A teacher of the æstheticism of the Lock Hospital." *Saturday Review.*

DESCRIPTIONS OF IBSEN'S ADMIRERS

"Lovers of prurience and dabblers in impropriety who are eager to gratify their illicit tastes under the pretence of art." *Evening Standard*. "Ninety-seven percent of the people who go to see Ghosts are nasty-minded people who find the discussion of nasty subjects to their taste in exact proportion to their nastiness." *Sporting and Dramatic News*. "The sexless . . . The unwomanly woman, the unsexed females, the whole army of unprepossessing cranks in petticoats . . . Educated and muck-ferreting dogs . . . Effeminate men and male women . . . They all of them— men and women alike—know that they are doing not only a nasty but an illegal thing . . . The Lord Chamberlain left them alone to wallow in Ghosts . . . Outside a silly clique, there is not the slightest interest in the Scandinavian humbug or all his works . . . A wave of human folly." *Truth*.[1]

[1] Outrageous as the above extracts now seem, I could make them appear quite moderate by setting beside them the hue and cry raised in New York in 1905 against a play of my own entitled Mrs. Warren's Profession. But there was a commercial reason for that. My play exposed what has since become known as the White Slave Traffic: that is, the organization of prostitution as a regular commercial industry yielding huge profits to capital invested in it, directly or indirectly, by "pillars of society." The attack on the play was so corrupt that the newspaper that took the lead in it was heavily fined shortly afterwards for trading in advertisements of the traffic. But the attack on Ghosts was, I believe, really disinterested and sincere on its moral side. No doubt Ibsen was virulently hated by some of the writers quoted, as all great and original artists are hated by contemporary mediocrity, which needs must hate the highest when it sees it. Our own mediocrities would abuse Ibsen as heartily as their fathers did if they were not young enough to have started with an entirely inculcated and unintelligent assumption that he is a classic, like Shakespear and Goethe, and therefore must not be abused and need not be understood. But

AN ENEMY OF THE PEOPLE, 1882

After this, the reader will understand the temper
in which Ibsen set about his next play, An Enemy of
the People, in which, having done sufficient execution
among the ordinary middle-class domestic and social
ideals, he puts his finger for a moment on commercial
political ideals. The play deals with a local majority
of middle-class people who are pecuniarily interested
in concealing the fact that the famous baths which
attract visitors to their town and customers to their
shops and hotels are contaminated by sewage. When
an honest doctor insists on exposing this danger, the
townspeople immediately disguise themselves ideally.
Feeling the disadvantage of appearing in their true
character as a conspiracy of interested rogues against
an honest man, they pose as Society, as The People, as
Democracy, as the solid Liberal Majority, and other
imposing abstractions, the doctor, in attacking them,
of course being thereby made an enemy of The People,
a danger to Society, a traitor to Democracy, an apostate from the great Liberal party, and so on. Only
those who take an active part in politics can appreciate
the grim fun of the situation, which, though it has an
intensely local Norwegian air, will be at once recognized as typical in England, not, perhaps, by the pro-

---

we have only to compare the frantic and indecent vituperation
quoted above with the mere disparagement and dislike expressed
towards Ibsen's other plays at the same period to perceive that
here Ibsen struck at something much deeper than the fancies of
critics as to the proper way to write plays. An ordinary farcical
comedy ridiculing Pastor Manders and making Alving out to be
a good fellow would have enlisted their sympathy at once, as
their tradition was distinctly "Bohemian." Their horror at
Ghosts is a striking proof of the worthlessness of mere Bohemianism, which has all the idle sentimentality and idolatry of
conventionality without any of its backbone of contract and
law. (1912.)

fessional literary critics, who are for the most part *fainéants* as far as political life is concerned, but certainly by everyone who has got as far as a seat on the committee of the most obscure Ratepayers' Association.

As An Enemy of the People contains one or two references to Democracy which are anything but respectful, it is necessary to examine Ibsen's criticism of it with precision. Democracy is really only an arrangement by which the governed are allowed to choose (as far as any choice is possible, which in capitalistic society is not saying much) the members of the representative bodies which control the executive. It has never been proved that this is the best arrangement; and it has been made effective only to the very limited extent short of which the dissatisfaction which it appeases might take the form af actual violence. Now when men had to submit to kings, they consoled themselves by making it an article of faith that the king was always right, idealizing him as a Pope, in fact. In the same way we who have to submit to majorities set up Voltaire's pope, *Monsieur Tout-le-monde*, and make it blasphemy against Democracy to deny that the majority is always right, although that, as Ibsen says, is a lie. It is a scientific fact that the majority, however eager it may be for the reform of old abuses, is always wrong in its opinion of new developments, or rather is always unfit for them (for it can hardly be said to be wrong in opposing developments for which it is not yet fit). The pioneer is a tiny minority of the force he heads; and so, though it is easy to be in a minority and yet be wrong, it is absolutely impossible to be in the majority and yet be right as to the newest social prospects. We should never progress at all if it were possible for each of us to stand still on democratic principles until we saw whither all the rest were moving, as our statesmen declare themselves bound to do when they are called upon to lead. Whatever clatter we may make for a time with our filing through feudal serf collars and kicking off old mercantilist fetters, we shall never march a step forward except at the heels of "the strongest man, he who is able to stand alone" and to turn his back on "the damned compact Liberal majority." All of which is no disparagement of parliaments and adult suffrage, but simply a wholesome reduction of them to their real place in the social economy as pure machinery: machinery which has absolutely no principles except the principles of mechanics, and no motive power in itself whatsoever. The idealization of public organizations is as dangerous as that of kings or priests. We need to be reminded that though there is in the world a vast number of buildings in which a certain ritual is conducted before crowds called congregations by a functionary called a priest, who is subject to a central council controlling all such functionaries on a few points, there is not therefore any such thing in the concrete as the ideal Catholic Church, nor ever was, nor ever will be. There may, too, be a highly elaborate organization of public affairs; but there is no such thing as the ideal State. There may be a combination of persons living by the practice of medicine, surgery, or physical or biological research; or by drawing up wills and leases, and preparing, pleading, or judging cases at law; or by painting pictures, writing books, and acting plays; or by serving in regiments and battle ships; or by manual labor or industrial service. But when any of these combinations, through its organizers or leaders, claims to deliver the Verdict of Science, or to act with the Authority of the Law, or to be as sacred as the Mission of Art, or to revenge criticisms of themselves as outrages on the Honor of His Majesty's Services, or to utter the Voice of Labor, there is urgent need for the guillotine, or whatever may be the mode in vogue of putting presumptuous persons in their proper place. All abstractions invested with collective consciousness or collective authority, set above the individual, and exacting duty from him on pretence of acting or thinking with greater validity than he, are man-eating idols red with human sacrifices.

This position must not be confounded with Anarchism, or the idealization of the repudiation of Governments. Ibsen did not refuse to pay the tax collector, but may be supposed to have regarded him, not as the vicar of an abstraction called THE STATE, but simply as the man sent round by a committee of citizens (mostly fools as far as Maximus the Mystic's Third Empire is concerned) to collect the money for the police or the paving and lighting of the streets.

THE WILD DUCK, 1884

After An Enemy of the People, Ibsen, as I have said, left the vulgar ideals for dead, and set about the exposure of those of the choicer spirits, beginning with the incorrigible idealists who had idealized his very self, and were becoming known as Ibsenites. His first move in this direction was such a tragi-comic slaughtering of sham Ibsenism that his astonished victims plaintively declared that The Wild Duck, as the new play was called, was a satire on his former works; whilst the pious, whom he had disappointed so severely by his interpretation of Brand, began to hope that he was coming back repentant to the fold. The household to which we are introduced in The Wild Duck is not, like Mrs. Alving's, a handsome one made miserable by superstitious illusions, but a shabby one made happy by romantic illusions. The only member of it who sees it as it really is is the wife, a good-natured Philistine who desires nothing better. The husband, a vain, petted, spoilt dawdler, believes that he is a delicate and high-souled man, devoting his life to redeeming his old father's name from the disgrace brought on it by

imprisonment for breach of the forest laws. This re-
demption he proposes to effect by making himself
famous as a great inventor some day when he has the
necessary inspiration. Their daughter, a girl in her
teens, believes intensely in her father and in the
promised invention. The disgraced grandfather cheers
himself by drink whenever he can get it; but his chief
resource is a wonderful garret full of rabbits and
pigeons. The old man has procured a number of
second-hand Christmas trees; and with these he has
turned the garret into a sort of toy forest, in which
he can play at bear hunting, which was one of the
sports of his youth and prosperity. The weapons employed in the hunting expeditions are a gun which
will not go off, and a pistol which occasionally brings
down a rabbit or a pigeon. A crowning touch is given
to the illusion by a wild duck, which, however, must
not be shot, as it is the special property of the girl, who
reads and dreams whilst her mother cooks, washes,
sweeps and carries on the photographic work which
is supposed to be the business of her husband. Mrs.
Ekdal does not appreciate Hjalmar's highly strung
sensitiveness of character, which is constantly suffering
agonizing jars from her vulgarity; but then she does
not appreciate that other fact that he is a lazy and idle
impostor. Downstairs there is a disgraceful clergyman
named Molvik, a hopeless drunkard; but even he respects himself and is tolerated because of a special illusion invented for him by another lodger, Dr. Relling,
upon whom the lesson of the household above has not
been thrown away. Molvik, says the doctor, must
break out into drinking fits because he is daimonic, an
imposing explanation which completely relieves the
reverend gentleman from the imputation of vulgar
tippling.

Into this domestic circle there comes a new lodger,
an idealist of the most advanced type. He greedily
swallows the daimonic theory of the clergyman's

drunkenness, and enthusiastically accepts the photographer as the high-souled hero he supposes himself to be; but he is troubled because the relations of the man and his wife do not constitute an ideal marriage. He happens to know that the woman, before her marriage, was the cast-off mistress of his own father; and because she has not told her husband this, he conceives her life as founded on a lie, like that of Bernick in Pillars of Society. He accordingly sets himself to work out the woman's salvation for her, and establish ideally frank relations between the pair, by simply blurting out the truth, and then asking them, with fatuous self-satisfaction, whether they do not feel much the better for it. This wanton piece of mischief has more serious results than a mere domestic scene. The husband is too weak to act on his bluster about outraged honor and the impossibility of his ever living with his wife again; and the woman is merely annoyed with the idealist for telling on her; but the girl takes the matter to heart and shoots herself. The doubt cast on her parentage, with her father's theatrical repudiation of her, destroy her ideal place in the home, and make her a source of discord there; so she sacrifices herself, thereby carrying out the teaching of the idealist mischief-maker, who has talked a good deal to her about the duty and beauty of self-sacrifice, without foreseeing that he might be taken in mortal earnest. The busybody thus finds that people cannot be freed from their failings from without. They must free themselves. When Nora is strong enough to live out of the doll's house, she will go out of it of her own accord if the door stands open; but if before that period you take her by the scruff of the neck and thrust her out, she will only take refuge in the next establishment of the kind that offers to receive her. Woman has thus two enemies to deal with: the old-fashioned one who wants to keep the door locked, and the new-fashioned one who wants to thrust her into the street before she is ready to go. In the cognate case of a hypocrite and liar like Bernick, exposing him is a mere police measure: he is none the less a liar and hypocrite when you have exposed him. If you want to make a sincere and truthful man of him, all you can wisely do is to remove what you can of the external obstacles to his exposing himself, and then wait for the operation of his internal impulse to confess. If he has no such impulse, then you must put up with him as he is. It is useless to make claims on him which he is not yet prepared to meet. Whether, like Brand, we make such claims because to refrain would be to compromise with evil, or, like Gregers Werle, because we think their moral beauty must recommend them at sight to every one, we shall alike incur Relling's impatient assurance that "life would be quite tolerable if we could only get rid of the confounded duns that keep on pestering us in our poverty with the claims of the ideal."

ROSMERSHOLM, 1886

Ibsen did not in The Wild Duck exhaust the subject of the danger of forming ideals for other people, and interfering in their lives with a view to enabling them to realize those ideals. Cases far more typical than that of the meddlesome lodger are those of the priest who regards the ennobling of mankind as a sort of trade process of which his cloth gives him a monopoly, and the clever woman who pictures a noble career for the man she loves, and devotes herself to helping him to achieve it. In Rosmersholm, the play with which Ibsen followed up The Wild Duck, there is an unpractical country parson, a gentleman of ancient stock, whose family has been for many years a centre of social influence. The tradition of that influence reinforces his priestly tendency to regard the ennoblement of the world as an external operation to be performed by himself; and the need of such ennoblement is very evident to him; for his nature is a fine one: he looks at the world with some dim prevision of "the third empire." He is married to a woman of passionately affectionate nature, who is very fond of him, but does not regard him as a regenerator of the human race. Indeed she does not share any of his dreams, and only acts as an extinguisher on the sacred fire of his idealism. He, she, her brother Kroll the headmaster, Kroll's wife, and their set, form a select circle of the best people in the place, comfortably orbited in our social system, and quite planetary in ascertained position and unimpeachable respectability. Into the orbit comes presently a wandering star, one Rebecca Gamvik, an unpropertied orphan, who has been allowed to read advanced books, and is a Freethinker and a Radical: things that disqualify a poor woman for admission to the Rosmer world. However, one must live somewhere; and as the Rosmer world is the only one in which an ambitious and cultivated woman can find powerful allies and educated companions, Rebecca, being both ambitious and cultivated, makes herself agreeable to the Rosmer circle with such success that the affectionate and impulsive but unintelligent Mrs. Rosmer becomes wildly fond of her, and is not content until she has persuaded her to come and live with them. Rebecca, then a mere adventuress fighting for a foothold in polite society (which has hitherto shewn itself highly indignant at her thrusting herself in where nobody has thought of providing room for her), accepts the offer all the more readily because she has taken the measure of Parson Rosmer, and formed the idea of playing upon his aspirations, and making herself a leader in politics and society by using him as a figurehead.

But now two difficulties arise. First, there is Mrs. Rosmer's extinguishing effect on her husband: an effect which convinces Rebecca that nothing can be done with him whilst his wife is in the way. Second—a contingency quite unallowed for in her provident calculations—she finds herself passionately enamored of him. The poor parson, too, falls in love with her; but he does not know it. He turns to the woman who understands him like a sunflower to the sun, and makes her his real friend and companion. The wife feels this soon enough; and he, quite unconscious of it, begins to think that her mind must be affected, since she has become so intensely miserable and hysterical about nothing—nothing that he can see. The truth is that she has come under the curse of Rebecca's ideal: she sees herself standing, a useless obstacle, between her husband and the woman he really loves, the woman who can help him to a glorious career. She cannot even be the mother in the household; for she is childless. Then comes Rebecca, fortified with a finely reasoned theory that Rosmer's future is staked against his wife's life, and says that it is better for all their sakes that she should quit Rosmersholm. She even hints that she must go at once if a grave scandal is to be avoided. Mrs. Rosmer, regarding a scandal in Rosmersholm as the most terrible thing that can happen, and seeing that it could be averted by the marriage of Rebecca and Rosmer if she were out of the way, writes a letter secretly to Rosmer's bitterest enemy, the editor of the local Radical paper, a man who has forfeited his moral reputation by an intrigue which Rosmer has pitilessly denounced. In this letter she implores him not to believe or publish any stories that he may hear about Rosmer, to the effect that he is in any way to blame for any thing that may happen to her. Then she sets Rosmer free to marry Rebecca, and to realize his ideals, by going out into the garden and throwing herself into the millstream that runs there.

Now follows a period of quiet mourning at Rosmersholm. Everybody except Rosmer suspects that Mrs. Rosmer was not mad, and guesses why she committed suicide. Only it would not do to compromise the aristocratic party by treating Rosmer as the Radical editor was treated. So the neighbors shut their eyes and condole with the bereaved clergyman; and the Radical editor holds his tongue because Radicalism is growing respectable, and he hopes, with Rebecca's help, to get Rosmer over to his side presently. Meanwhile the unexpected has again happened to Rebecca. Her passion is worn out; but in the long days of mourning she has found the higher love; and it is now for Rosmer's own sake that she urges him to become a man of action, and brood no more over the dead. When his friends start a Conservative paper and ask him to become editor, she induces him to reply by declaring himself a Radical and Freethinker. To his utter amazement, the result is, not an animated discussion of his views, but just such an attack on his home life and private conduct as he had formerly made on those of the Radical editor. His friends tell him plainly that the compact of silence is broken by his defection, and that there will be no mercy for the traitor to the party. Even the Radical editor not only refuses to publish the fact that his new ally is a Freethinker (which would destroy all his social weight as a Radical recruit), but brings up the dead woman's letter as a proof that the attack is sufficiently well-founded to make it unwise to go too far. Rosmer, who at first had been simply shocked that men whom he had always honored as gentlemen should descend to such hideous calumny, now sees that he really did love Rebecca, and is indeed guilty of his wife's death. His first impulse is to shake off the spectre of the dead woman by marrying Rebecca; but she, knowing that the guilt is hers, puts that temptation behind her and refuses. Then, as he thinks it all over, his dream of ennobling the world slips away from him: such work can only be done by a man conscious of his own innocence. To save him from despair, Rebecca makes a great sacrifice. She "gives him back his innocence" by confessing how she drove his wife to kill herself; and, as the confession is made in the presence of Kroll, she ascribes the whole plot to her ambition, and says not a word of her passion. Rosmer, confounded as he realizes what helpless puppets they have all been in the hands of this clever woman, for the moment misses the point that unscrupulous ambition, though it explains her crime, does not account for her confession. He turns his back on her and leaves the house with Kroll. She quietly packs up her trunk, and is about to vanish from Rosmersholm without another word when he comes back alone to ask why she confessed. She tells him why, offering him her self-sacrifice as a proof that his power of ennobling others was no vain dream, since it is his companionship that has changed her from the selfish adventuress she was to the devoted woman she has just proved herself to be. But he has lost his faith in himself, and cannot believe her. The proof seems to him subtle, artful: he cannot forget that she duped him by flattering this very weakness of his before. Besides, he knows now that it is not true: people are not ennobled from without. She has no more to say; for she can think of no further proof. But he has thought of an unanswerable one. Dare she make all doubt impossible by sacrificing her share in his future in the only absolutely final way: that is, by doing for his sake what his wife did? She asks what would happen if she had the heart and the will to do it. "Then," he replies, "I should have to believe in you. I should recover my faith in my mission. Faith in my power to ennoble human souls. Faith in the human soul's power to attain nobility." "You shall have your faith again," she answers. At this pass the inner truth of the situation comes out;

and the thin veil of a demand for proof, with its monstrous sequel of asking the woman to kill herself in order to restore the man's good opinion of himself, falls away. What is really driving Rosmer is the superstition of expiation by sacrifice. He sees that when Rebecca goes into the millstream he must go too. And he speaks his real mind in the words, "There is no judge over us: therefore we must do justice upon ourselves." But the woman's soul is free of this to the end; for when she says, "I am under the power of the Rosmersholm view of life *now*. What I have sinned it is fit I should expiate," we feel in that speech a protest against the Rosmersholm view of life: the view that denied her right to live and be happy from the first, and now at the end, even in denying its God, exacts her life as a vain blood-offering for its own blindness. The woman has the higher light: she goes to her death out of fellowship with the man who is driven thither by the superstition which has destroyed his will. The story ends with his taking her solemnly as his wife, and casting himself with her into the millstream.

It is unnecessary to repeat here what is said on page 37 as to the vital part played in this drama by the evolution of the lower into the higher love. Peer Gynt, during the prophetic episode in his career, shocks the dancing girl Anitra into a remonstrance by comparing himself to a cat. He replies, with his wisest air, that from the standpoint of love there is perhaps not so much difference between a tomcat and a prophet as she may imagine. The number of critics who have entirely missed the point of Rebecca's transfiguration seems to indicate that the majority of men, even among critics of dramatic poetry, have not got beyond Peer Gynt's opinion in this matter. No doubt they would not endorse it as a definitely stated proposition, aware, as they are, that there is a poetic convention to the

contrary. But if they fail to recognize the only possible alternative proposition when it is not only stated
in so many words by Rebecca West, but when without it her conduct dramatically contradicts her character—when they even complain of the contradiction as
a blemish on the play, I am afraid there can be no
further doubt that the extreme perplexity into which
the first performance of Rosmersholm in England
plunged the Press was due entirely to the prevalence of
Peer Gynt's view of love among the dramatic critics.

THE LADY FROM THE SEA, 1888

Ibsen's next play, though it deals with the old theme,
does not insist on the power of ideals to kill, as the
two previous plays do. It rather deals with the origin
of ideals in unhappiness, in dissatisfaction with the
real. The subject of The Lady from the Sea is the
most poetic fancy imaginable. A young woman,
brought up on the sea-coast, marries a respectable
doctor, a widower, who idolizes her and places her in
his household with nothing to do but dream and be
made much of by everybody. Even the housekeeping is
done by her stepdaughter: she has no responsibility,
no care, and no trouble. In other words, she is an idle,
helpless, utterly dependent article of luxury. A man
turns red at the thought of being such a thing; but
he thoughtlessly accepts a pretty and fragile-looking
woman in the same position as a charming natural
picture. The lady from the sea feels an indefinite want
in her life. She reads her want into all other lives, and
comes to the conclusion that man once had to choose
whether he would be a land animal or a creature of
the sea; and that having chosen the land, he has carried
about with him ever since a secret sorrow for the element he has forsaken. The dissatisfaction that gnaws

her is, as she interprets it, this desperate longing for the sea. When her only child dies and leaves her without the work of a mother to give her a valid place in the world, she yields wholly to her longing, and no longer cares for her husband, who, like Rosmer, begins to fear that she is going mad.

At last a seaman appears and claims her as his wife on the ground that they went years before through a rite which consisted of their marrying the sea by throwing their rings into it. This man, who had to fly from her in the old time because he killed his captain, and who fills her with a sense of dread and mystery, seems to her to embody the mystic attraction the sea has for her. She tells her husband that she must go away with the seaman. Naturally the doctor expostulates—declares that he cannot for her own sake let her do so mad a thing. She replies that he can only prevent her by locking her up, and asks him what satisfaction it will be to him to have her body under lock and key whilst her heart is with the other man. In vain he urges that he will only keep her under restraint until the seaman goes—that he must not, dare not, allow her to ruin herself. Her argument remains unanswerable. The seaman openly declares that she will come; so that the distracted husband asks him does he suppose he can force her from her home. To this the seaman replies that, on the contrary, unless she comes of her own free will there is no satisfaction to him in her coming at all: the unanswerable argument again. She echoes it by demanding her freedom to choose. Her husband must cry off his law-made and Church-made bargain; renounce his claim to the fulfilment of her vows; and leave her free to go back to the sea with her old lover. Then the doctor, with a heavy heart, drops his prate about his heavy responsibility for her actions, and throws the responsibility on her by crying off as she demands. The moment she feels herself a free and responsible woman, all her childish fancies vanish: the seaman becomes simply an old acquaintance whom she no longer cares for; and the doctor's affection produces its natural effect. In short, she says No to the seaman, and takes over the housekeeping keys from her stepdaughter without any further maunderings over that secret sorrow for the abandoned sea.

It should be noted here that Ellida [call her Eleeda], The Lady from the Sea, seems more fantastic to English readers than to Norwegian ones. The same thing is true of many other characters drawn by Ibsen, notably Peer Gynt, who, if born in England, would certainly not have been a poet and metaphysician as well as a blackguard and a speculator. The extreme type of Norwegian, as depicted by Ibsen, imagines himself doing wonderful things, but does nothing. He dreams as no Englishman dreams, and drinks to make himself dream the more, until his effective will is destroyed, and he becomes a broken-down, disreputable sot, carrying about the tradition that he is a hero, and discussing himself on that assumption. Although the number of persons who dawdle their life away over fiction in England must be frightful, and is probably increasing, yet their talk is not the talk of Ulric Brendel, Rosmer, Ellida, or Peer Gynt; and it is for this reason that Rosmersholm and The Lady from the Sea strike English audiences as more fantastic and less literal than A Doll's House and the plays in which the leading figures are men and women of action, though to a Norwegian there is probably no difference in this respect.

HEDDA GABLER, 1890

Hedda Gabler has no ethical ideals at all, only romantic ones. She is a typical nineteenth century figure, falling into the abyss between the ideals which do not impose on her and the realities she has not yet discovered. The result is that though she has imagination, and an intense appetite for beauty, she has no conscience, no conviction: with plenty of cleverness, energy, and personal fascination she remains mean, envious, insolent, cruel in protest against others' happiness, fiendish in her dislike of inartistic people and things, a bully in reaction from her own cowardice. Hedda's father, a general, is a widower. She has the traditions of the military caste about her; and these narrow her activities to the customary hunt for a socially and pecuniarily eligible husband. She makes the acquaintance of a young man of genius who, prohibited by an ideal-ridden society from taking his pleasures except where there is nothing to restrain him from excess, is going to the bad in search of his good, with the usual consequences. Hedda is intensely curious about the side of life which is forbidden to her, and in which powerful instincts, absolutely ignored and condemned in her circle, steal their satisfaction. An odd intimacy springs up between the inquisitive girl and the rake. Whilst the general reads the paper in the afternoon, Lövborg and Hedda have long conversations in which he decribes to her all his disreputable adventures. Although she is the questioner, she never dares to trust him: all the questions are indirect; and the responsibility for his interpretations rests on him alone. Hedda has no conviction whatever that these conversations are disgraceful; but she will not risk a fight with society on the point: it is easier to practise hypocrisy, the homage that truth pays to falsehood, than to endure ostracism. When he proceeds to make advances to her, Hedda has again no conviction that it would be wrong for her to gratify his instinct and her own; so that she is confronted with the alternative of sinning against herself and him, or sinning against social ideals in which she has no faith. Making the coward's choice, she carries it out with the utmost bravado, threatening Lövborg with one of her father's pistols, and driving him out of the house with all that ostentation of outraged purity which is the instinctive defence of women to whom chastity is not natural, much as libel actions are mostly brought by persons concerning whom libels are virtually, if not technically, justifiable.

Hedda, deprived of her lover, now finds that a life of conformity without faith involves something more terrible than the utmost ostracism: to wit, boredom. This scourge, unknown among revolutionists, is the curse which makes the security of respectability as dust in the balance against the unflagging interest of rebellion, and which forces society to eke out its harmless resources for killing time by licensing gambling, gluttony, hunting, shooting, coursing, and other vicious distractions for which even idealism has no disguise. These licenses, being expensive, are available only for people who have more than enough money to keep up appearances; and as Hedda's father, being in the army instead of in commerce, is too poor to leave her much more than the pistols, her boredom is only mitigated by dancing, at which she gains much admiration, but no substantial offers of marriage.

At last she has to find somebody to support her. A good-natured mediocrity of a professor is the best that is to be had; and though she regards him as a member of an inferior class, and despises almost to loathing his family circle of two affectionate old aunts and the inevitable general servant who has helped to bring him up, she marries him *faute de mieux*, and immediately proceeds to wreck this prudent provision for her livelihood by accommodating his income to her expenditure instead of accommodating her expenditure to his income. Her nature so rebels against the whole

sordid transaction that the prospect of bearing a child
to her husband drives her almost frantic, since it will
not only expose her to the intimate solicitude of his
aunts in the course of a derangement of her health in
which she can see nothing that is not repulsive and
humiliating, but will make her one of his family in
earnest.

To amuse herself in these galling circumstances, she
forms an underhand alliance with a visitor who belongs
to her old set, an elderly gallant who quite understands
how little she cares for her husband, and proposes a
ménage à trois to her. She consents to his coming there
and talking to her as he pleases behind her husband's
back; but she keeps her pistols in reserve in case he
becomes seriously importunate. He, on the other hand,
tries to get some hold over her by placing her husband
under pecuniary obligations, as far as he can do it
without being out of pocket.

Meanwhile Lövborg is drifting to disgrace by the
nearest way: drink. In due time he descends from lec-
turing at the university on the history of civilization
to taking a job in an out-of-the-way place as tutor to
the little children of Sheriff Elvsted. This functionary,
on being left a widower with a number of children,
marries their governess, finding that she will cost him
less and be bound to do more for him as his wife. As
for her, she is too poor to dream of refusing such a
settlement in life. When Lövborg comes, his society is
heaven to her. He does not dare tell her about his dis-
sipations; but he tells her about his unwritten books,
which he never discussed with Hedda. She does not
dare to remonstrate with him for drinking; but he gives
it up as soon as he sees that it shocks her. Just as Mr.
Fearing, in Bunyan's story, was in a way the bravest of
the pilgrims, so this timid and unfortunate Mrs. Elvsted
trembles her way to a point at which Lövborg, quite
reformed, publishes one book which makes him cele-

brated for the moment, and completes another, fair-copied in her handwriting, to which he looks for a solid position as an original thinker. But he cannot now stay tutoring Elvsted's children; so off he goes to town with his pockets full of the money the published book has brought him. Left once more in her old lonely plight, knowing that without her Lövborg will probably relapse into dissipation, and that without him her life will not be worth living, Mrs. Elvsted must either sin against herself and him or against the institution of marriage under which Elvsted purchased his house-keeper. It never occurs to her that she has any choice. She knows that her action will count as "a dreadful thing"; but she sees that she must go; and accordingly Elvsted finds himself without a wife and his children without a governess, and so disappears unpitied from the story.

Now it happens that Hedda's husband, Jörgen Tes-man, is an old friend and competitor (for academic honors) of Lövborg, and also that Hedda was a school-fellow of Mrs. Elvsted, or Thea, as she had better now be called. Thea's first business is to find out where Lövborg is; for hers is no preconcerted elopement: she has hurried to town to keep Lövborg away from the bottle, a design she dare not hint at to himself. Accordingly, the first thing she does in town is to call on the Tesmans, who have just returned from their honeymoon, to beg them to invite Lövborg to their house so as to keep him in good company. They consent, with the result that the two pairs are brought together under the same roof, and the tragedy begins to work itself out.

Hedda's attitude now demands a careful analysis. Lövborg's experience with Thea has enlightened his judgment of Hedda; and as he is, in his gifted way, an arrant *poseur* and male coquet, he immediately tries to get on romantic terms with her (for have they not "a

past"?) by impressing her with the penetrating criticism that she is and always was a coward. She admits
that the virtuous heroics with the pistol were pure
cowardice; but she is still so void of any other standard
of conduct than conformity to the conventional ideals,
that she thinks her cowardice consisted in not daring
to be wicked. That is, she thinks that what she actually
did was the right thing; and since she despises herself
for doing it, and feels that he also rightly despises her
for doing it, she gets a passionate feeling that what is
wanted is the courage to do wrong. This unlooked-for
reaction of idealism, this monstrous but very common
setting-up of wrong-doing as an ideal, and of the
wrongdoer as hero or heroine *qua* wrongdoer, leads
Hedda to conceive that when Lövborg tried to seduce
her he was a hero, and that in allowing Thea to reform
him he has played the recreant. In acting on this mis-
conception she is restrained by no consideration for
any of the rest. Like all people whose lives are valueless,
she has no more sense of the value of Lövborg's or
Tesman's or Thea's lives than a railway shareholder has
of the value of a shunter's. She gratifies her intense
jealousy of Thea by deliberately taunting Lövborg into
breaking loose from her influence by joining a carouse
at which he not only loses his manuscript, but finally
gets into the hands of the police through behaving out-
rageously in the house of a disreputable woman whom
he accuses of stealing it, not knowing that it has been
picked up by Tesman and handed to Hedda for safe
keeping. Now Hedda's jealousy of Thea is not jealousy
of her bodily fascination: at that Hedda can beat her.
It is jealousy of her power of making a man of Lövborg,
of her part in his life as a man of genius. The manuscript which Tesman gives to Hedda to lock up safely
is in Thea's handwriting. It is the fruit of Lövborg's
union with Thea: he himself speaks of it as "their
child." So when he turns his despair to romantic account

by coming to the two women and making a tragic scene, telling Thea that he has cast the manuscript, torn into a thousand pieces, out upon the fiord; and then, when she is gone, telling Hedda that he has brought "the child" to a house of ill-fame and lost it there, she, deceived by his posing, and thirsting to gain faith in the beauty of her own influence over him from a heroic deed of some sort, makes him a present of one of her pistols, only begging him to "do it beautifully," by which she means that he is to kill himself in some manner that will make his suicide a romantic memory and an imaginative luxury to her for ever. He takes it unblushingly, and leaves her with the air of a man who is looking his last on earth. But the moment he is out of sight of his audience, he goes back to the house where he still supposes the manuscript to lie stolen, and there renews the wrangle of the night before, using the pistol to threaten the woman, with the result that he gets shot in the abdomen, leaving the weapon to fall into the hands of the police. Meanwhile Hedda deliberately burns "the child." Then comes her elderly gallant to disgust her with the unromantically ugly details of the deed which Lövborg promised her to do so beautifully, and to make her understand that he himself has now got her into his power by his ability to identify the pistol. She must either be the slave of this man, or else face the scandal of the connection of her name at the inquest with a squalid debauch ending in a murder. Thea, too, is not crushed by Lövborg's death. Ten minutes after she has received the news with a cry of heartfelt loss, she sits down with Tesman to reconstruct "the child" from the old notes she has piously pre-served. Over the congenial task of collecting and ar-ranging another man's ideas Tesman is perfectly happy, and forgets his beautiful Hedda for the first time. Thea the trembler is still mistress of the situation, holding the dead Lövborg, gaining Tesman, and leaving Hedda to her elderly admirer, who smoothly remarks that he will answer for Mrs. Tesman not being bored whilst her husband is occupied with Thea in putting the pieces of the book together. However, he has again reckoned without General Gabler's second pistol. She shoots herself then and there; and so the story ends.

THE LAST FOUR PLAYS

DOWN AMONG THE DEAD MEN

IBSEN now lays down the completed task of warning the world against its idols and anti-idols, and passes into the shadow of death, or rather into the splendor of his sunset glory; for his magic is extraordinarily potent in these four plays, and his purpose more powerful. And yet the shadow of death is here; for all four, except Little Eyolf, are tragedies of the dead, deserted and mocked by the young who are still full of life. The Master Builder is a dead man before the curtain rises: the breaking of his body to pieces in the last act by its fall from the tower is rather the impatient destruction of a ghost of whose delirious whisperings Nature is tired than of one who still counts among the living. Borkman and the two women, his wife and her sister, are not merely dead: they are buried; and the creatures we hear and see are only their spirits in torment. "Never dream of life again," says Mrs. Borkman to her husband: "lie quiet where you are." And the last play of all is frankly called When We Dead Awaken. Here the quintessence of Ibsenism reaches its final distillation; morality and reformation give place to mortality and resurrection; and the next event is the death of Ibsen himself: he, too, creeping ghost-like through the blackening mental darkness until he reaches his actual grave, and can no longer make Europe cry with pity by sitting

117

at a copybook, like a child, trying to learn again how to write, only to find that divine power gone for ever from his dead hand. He, the crustiest, grimmest hero since Beethoven, could not die like him, shaking his fist at the thunder and alive to the last: he must follow the path he had traced for Solness and Borkman, and survive himself. But as these two were dreamers to the last, and never so luminous in their dreams as when they could no longer put the least of them into action; so we may believe that when Ibsen could no longer remember the alphabet, or use a dictionary, his soul may have been fuller than ever before of the unspeakable. Do not snivel, reader, over the contrast he himself drew between the man who was once the greatest writer in the world, and the child of seventy-six trying to begin again at pothooks and hangers. Depend on it, whilst there was anything left of him at all there was enough of his iron humor to grin as widely as the skeleton with the hourglass who was touching him on the shoulder.

THE MASTER BUILDER, 1892

Halvard Solness is a dead man who has been a brilliantly successful builder, and, like the greatest builders, his own architect. He is sometimes in the sublime delirium that precedes bodily death, and sometimes in the horror that varies the splendors of delirium. He is mortally afraid of young rivals; of the younger generation knocking at the door. He has built churches with high towers (much as Ibsen built great historical dramas in verse). He has come to the end of that and built "homes for human beings" (much as Ibsen took to writing prose plays of modern life). He has come to the end of that too, as men do at the end of their lives; and now he must take to dead men's architecture, the building of castles in the air. Castles in the air are the residences not only of those who have finished their lives, but of those who have not yet begun them. Another peculiarity of castles in the air is that they are so beautiful and so wonderful that human beings are not good enough to live in them: therefore when you look round you for somebody to live with you in your castle in the air, you find nobody glorious enough for that sanctuary. So you resort to the most dangerous of all the varieties of idolization: the idolization of the person you are most in love with; and you take him or her to live with you in your castle. And as imaginative young people, because they are young, have no illusions about youth, whilst old people, because they are old, have no illusions about age, elderly gentlemen very often idolize adolescent girls, and adolescent girls idolize elderly gentlemen. When the idolization is not reciprocal, the idolizer runs terrible risks if the idol is selfish and unscrupulous. Cases of girls enslaved by elderly gentlemen whose scrupulous respect for their maiden purity is nothing but an excuse for getting a quantity of secretarial or domestic service out of them that is limited only by their physical endurance, without giving them anything in return, are not at all so rare as they would be if the theft of a woman's youth and devotion were as severely condemned by public opinion as the comparatively amiable and negligible theft of a few silver spoons and forks. On the other hand doting old gentlemen are duped and ruined by designing young women who care no more for them than a Cornish fisherman cares for a conger eel. But sometimes, when the two natures are poetic, we have scenes of Bettina and Goethe, which are perhaps wholesome as well as pleasant for both parties when they are good enough and sensible enough to face the inexorable on the side of age and to recognize the impossible on the side of youth. On these conditions, old gentlemen are indulged in fancies for poetic little girls; and the poetic little girls have their emotions and imaginations satisfied harmlessly until they find a suitable mate.

But the master builder, though he gets into just such a situation, does not get out of it so cheaply, because he is not outwardly an old, or even a very elderly gentleman. "He is a man no longer young, but healthy and vigorous, with closely cut curly hair, dark moustache, and dark thick eyebrows." Also he is daimonic, not sham daimonic like Molvik in The Wild Duck, but really daimonic, with luck, a star, and mystic "helpers and servers" who find the way through the maze of life for him. In short, a very fascinating man, whom nobody, himself least of all, could suspect of having shot his bolt and being already dead. Therefore a man for whom a girl's castle in the air is a very dangerous place, as she may easily thrust upon him adventures that would tax the prime of an unexhausted man, and are mere delirious madness for a spent one.

Grasp this situation and you will be able to follow a performance of The Master Builder without being puzzled; though to the unprepared theatregoer it is a bewildering business. You see Solness in his office, ruthlessly exploiting the devotion of the girl secretary Kaia, who idolizes him, and giving her nothing in return but a mesmerizing word occasionally. You see him with equal ruthlessness apparently, but really with the secret terror of "the priest who slew the slayer and shall himself be slain," trying to suppress a young rival who is as yet only a draughtsman in his employment. To keep the door shut against the younger generation already knocking at it: that is all he can do now, except build castles in the air; for, as I have said, the effective part of the man is dead. Then there is his wife, who, knowing that he is failing in body and mind, can do nothing but look on in helpless terror. She cannot make a happy home for Solness, because her own happiness has been sacrificed to his. For they began their family life in an old house that was part of her property: the sort of house that may be hallowed by old family associations and memories of childhood, but that it pays the speculative builder to pull down and replace by rows of villas. Now the ambitious Solness knows this but dares not propose such a thing to his wife, who cherishes all the hallowing associations, and even keeps her dolls: nine lovely dolls, feeling them "under her heart, like little unborn children." Everything in the house is precious to her: the old silk dresses, the lace, the portraits. Solness knows that to touch these would be tearing her heart up by the roots. So he says nothing; does nothing; only notes a crack in the old chimney which should be repaired if the house is to be safe against fire, and does not repair it. Instead, he pictures to himself a fire, with his wife out in the sledge with his two children, and nothing but charred ruins facing her when she returns; but what matter, since the children have escaped and are still with her? He even calls upon his helpers and servers to consider whether this vision might not become a reality. And it does. The house is burnt; the villas rise on its site and cover the park; and Halvard Solness becomes rich and successful.

But the helpers and servers have not stuck to the program for all that. The fire did not come from the crack in the chimney when all the domestic fires were blazing. It came at night when the fires were low, and began in a cupboard quite away from the chimney. It came when Mrs. Solness and the children were in bed. It shattered the mother's health; it killed the children she was nursing; it devoured the portraits and the silk dresses and the old lace; it burnt the nine lovely dolls; and it broke the heart under which the dolls had lain like little unborn children. That was the price of the master builder's success. He is married to a dead woman; and he is trying to atone by building her a new villa: a new tomb to replace the old home; for he is gnawed with remorse.

But the fire was not only a good building speculation: it also led to his obtaining commissions to build churches. And one triumphant day, when he was cele-

brating the completion of the giant tower he had added
to the old church at Lysanger, it suddenly flashed on
him that his house had been burnt, his wife's life laid
waste, and his own happiness destroyed, so that he
might become a builder of churches. Now it happens
that one of his difficulties as a builder is that he had a
bad head for heights, and cannot venture even on a
second floor balcony. Yet in the fury of that thought
he mounts to the pinnacle of his tower, and there, face
to face with God, who has, he feels, wasted the wife's
gift of building up the souls of little children to make
the husband a builder of steeples, he declares that he
will never set hand to church-building again, and will
henceforth build nothing but homes for happier men
than he. Which vow he keeps, only to find that the
home, too, is a devouring idol, and that men and women
have no longer any use for it.

In spite of his excitement, he very nearly breaks his
neck after all; for among the crowd below there is a
little devil of a girl who waves a white scarf and makes
his head swim. This tiny animal is no other than the
younger stepdaughter of Ellida, The Lady from the
Sea, Hilda Wangel, of whose taste for "thrilling" sen-
sations we had a glimpse in that play. On the same
evening Solness is entertained at a club banquet, in
consequence of which he is not in the most responsible
condition when he returns to sup at the house of Dr.
Wangel, who is putting him up for the night. He meets
the imp there; thinks her like a little princess in her
white dress; kisses her; and promises her to come back
in ten years and carry her off to the kingdom of Oran-
gia. Perhaps it is only just to mention that he stoutly
denies these indiscretions afterwards; though he admits
that when he wishes something to happen between
himself and somebody else, the somebody else always
imagines it actually has happened.

The play begins ten years after the climbing of the
tower. The younger generation knocks at the door with

a vengeance. Hilda, now a vigorous young woman, and a great builder of castles in the air, bursts in on him and demands her kingdom; and very soon she sends him up to a tower again (the tower of the new house) and waves her scarf to him as madly as ever. This time he really does break his neck; and so the story ends.

LITTLE EYOLF, 1894

Though the most mischievous ideals are social ideals which have become institutions, laws, and creeds, yet their evil must come to a personal point before they can strike down the individual. Jones is not struck down by an ideal in the abstract, but by Smith making monstrous claims or inflicting monstrous injuries on him in the name of an ideal. And it is fair to add that the ideals are sometimes beneficent, and their repudiation sometimes cruel. For ideals are in practice not so much matters of conscience as excuses for doing what we like; and thus it happens that of two people worshipping the same ideals, one will be a detestable tyrant and the other a kindly and helpful friend of mankind. What makes the bad side of idealism so dangerous is that wicked people are allowed to commit crimes in the name of the ideal that would not be tolerated for a moment as open devilment. Perhaps the worst, because the commonest and most intimate cases, are to be found in family life. Even during the Reign of Terror, the chances of any particular Frenchman or Frenchwoman being guillotined were so small as to be negligible. Under Nero a Christian was far safer from being smeared with pitch and set on fire than he was from domestic trouble. If the private lives that have been wasted by idealistic persecution could be recorded and set against the public martyrdoms and slaughterings and torturings and imprisonments, our millions of private Neros and Torquemadas and Calvins, Bloody

Maries and Cleopatras and Semiramises, would eclipse the few who have come to the surface of history by the accident of political or ecclesiastical conspicuousness.

Thus Ibsen, at the beginning of his greatness, shewed us Brand sacrificing his wife; and this was only the first of a series of similar exhibitions, ending, so far, in Solness sacrificing his wife and being himself sacrificed to a girl's enthusiasm. And he brings Solness to the point of rebelling furiously against the tyranny of his wife's ideal of home, and declaring that "building homes for happy human beings is not worth a rap: men are not happy in these homes: I should not have been happy in such a home if I had had one." It is not surprising to find that Little Eyolf is about such a home.

This home clearly cannot be a working-class home. And here let it be said that the comparative indifference of the working class to Ibsen's plays is neither Ibsen's fault nor that of the working class. To the man who works for his living in modern society home is not the place where he lives, nor his wife the woman he lives with. Home is the roof under which he sleeps and eats; and his wife is the woman who makes his bed, cooks his meals, and looks after their children when they are neither in school nor in the streets, or who at least sees that the servants do these things. The man's work keeps him from home from eight to twelve hours a day. He is unconscious through sleep for another eight hours. Then there is the public house and the club. There is eating, washing, dressing, playing with the children or the dog, entertaining or visiting friends, reading, and pursuing hobbies such as gardening and the like. Obviously the home ideal cannot be tested fully under these conditions, which enable a married pair to see less and know less of one another than they do of those who work side by side with them. It is in the propertied class only that two people can really live together and devote themselves to one another if they want to. There are certain businesses which men and women

can conduct jointly, and certain professions which
men can pursue at home; and in these the strain of
idealism on marriage is more severe than when the two
work separately. But the full strain comes on with the
modern unearned income from investments, which does
not involve even the management of an estate. And it
is under this full strain that Ibsen tests it in Little Eyolf.

Shakespear, in a flash of insight which has puzzled
many commentators, and even set them proposing al-
terations of a passage which they found unthinkable,
has described one of his characters as "a fellow almost
damned in a fair wife." There is no difficulty or ob-
scurity about this phrase at all: you have only to look
round at the men who have ventured to marry very
fascinating women to see that most of them are not
merely "almost damned" but wholly damned. Allmers,
in Little Eyolf, is a fellow almost damned in a fair wife.
She, Rita Allmers, has brought him "gold and green
forests" (a reminiscence from an early play called The
Feast at Solhoug), and not only troubles and uncen-
tres him as only a woman can trouble and uncentre a
man who is susceptible to her bodily attraction, but is
herself furiously and jealously in love with him. In
short, they form the ideal home of romance; and it
would be hard to find a compacter or more effective
formula for a small private hell. The "almost damned"
are commonly saved by the fact that the devotion is
usually on one side only, and that the lovely lady (or
gentleman; for a woman almost damned in a fair husband is also a common object in domestic civilization),
if she has only one husband, relieves the boredom of
his devotion by having fifty courtiers. But Rita will
neither share Allmers with anyone else nor be shared.
He must be wholly and exclusively hers; and she must
be wholly and exclusively his. By her gold and green
forests she snatches him from his work as a schoolmaster and imprisons him in their house, where the
poor wretch pretends to occupy himself by writing a

book on Human Responsibility, and forming the character of their son, little Eyolf. For your male sultana takes himself very seriously indeed, as do most sultanas and others who are so closely shut up with their own vanities and appetites that they think the world a little thing to be moulded and arranged at their silly pleasure like a lump of plasticine. Rita is jealous of the book, and hates it not only because Allmers occupies himself with it instead of with her, but talks about it to his half-sister Asta, of whom she is of course also jealous. She is jealous of little Eyolf, and hates him too, because he comes between her and her prey.

One day, when the baby child is lying on the table, they have an amorous fit and forget all about him. He falls off the table and is crippled for life. He and his crutch become thenceforth a standing reproach to them. They hate themselves; they hate each other; they hate him; their atmosphere of ideal conjugal love breeds hate at every turn: hatred masquerading as a loving bond that has been drawn closer and sanctified by their common misfortune. After ten years of this hideous slavery the man breaks loose: actually insists on going for a short trip into the mountains by himself. It is true that he reassures Rita by coming back before his time; but her conclusion that this was because he could not abstain from her society is rudely shattered by his conduct on his return. She dresses herself beautifully to receive him, and makes the seraglio as delightful as possible for their reunion; but he purposely arrives tired out, and takes refuge in the sleep of exhaustion, without a caress. As she says, quoting a popular poem when reproaching him for this afterwards, "There stood your champagne and you tasted it not." It soon appears that he has come to loathe his champagne, and that the escape into the mountains has helped him to loathe his situation to some extent, even to discovering the absurdity of his book on Human Responsibility, and the cruelty of his educational experiments on Eyolf. In future he is going to make Eyolf "an open air little boy," which of course involves being a good deal in the open air with him, and out of the seraglio. Then the woman's hatred of the child unveils itself; and she openly declares what she really feels as to this little creature, with its "evil eyes," that has come between them.

At this point, very opportunely, comes the Rat Wife, who, like the Pied Piper, clears away rats for a consideration. Has Rita any little gnawing things she wants to get rid of? Here, it seems, is a helper and server for Rita. The Rat Wife's method is to bewitch the rats so that when she rows out to sea they follow her and are drowned. She describes this with a heart-breaking poetry that frightens Rita, who makes Allmers send her away. But a helper and server is not so easily exorcized. Rita's little gnawing thing, Eyolf, has come under the spell; and when the Rat Wife rows out to sea, he follows her and is drowned.

The family takes the event in a very proper spirit. Horror, lamentation, shrieks and tears, and all the customary homages to death and attestations of bereavement are duly and even sincerely gone through; for the shock of such an accident makes us all human for a moment. But next morning Allmers finds some difficulty in keeping it up, miserable as he is. He finds himself forgetting about Eyolf for several minutes, and thinking about other things, even about his breakfast; and in his idealistic self-devotion to artificial attitudes he reproaches himself and tries to force himself to keep thinking of Eyolf and being overwhelmed with grief about him. Besides, it is an excuse for avoiding his wife. The revulsion against his slavery to her has made her presence unbearable to him. He can bear nobody but his half-sister Asta, whose relation to him is a most blessed comfort and relief because their blood kinship excludes from it all the torment and slavery of his relation to Rita. But this consolation is presently withdrawn; for Asta has just discovered, in some old correspondence, convincing proofs that she is not related to him at all; and the effect of the discovery has been to remove the inhibition which has hitherto limited her strong affection for him; so that she now perceives that she must leave him. Hitherto, she has refused, for his sake, the offers of Borgheim, an engineer who wants to marry her, but who, like Rita, wants to take her away and make her exclusively his own; for he, too, cannot share with anyone. And though both Allmers and Rita implore her to stay, dreading now nothing so much as being left alone with one another, she knows that she cannot stay innocently, and accepts the engineer and vanishes lest a worse thing should befall.

And now Rita has her man all to herself. Eyolf dead, Asta gone, the Book on Human Responsibility thrown into the waste paper basket: there are no more rivals now, no more distractions: the field is clear for the ideal union of "two souls with but a single thought, two hearts that beat as one." The result may be imagined.

The situation is insufferable from the beginning. Allmers' attempts to avoid seeing or speaking to Rita are of course impracticable. Equally impracticable are their efforts to behave kindly to one another. They are presently at it hammer and tongs, each tearing the mask from the other's grief for the child, and leaving it exposed as their remorse: hers for having jealously hated Eyolf: his for having sacrificed him to his passion for Rita, and to the schoolmasterly vanity and folly which sees in the child nothing more than the vivisector sees in a guinea-pig: something to experiment on with a view to rearranging the world to suit his own little ideas. If ever two cultivated souls of the propertied middle class were stripped naked and left bankrupt, these two are. They cannot bear to live; and yet they are forced to confess that they dare not kill themselves.

The solution of their problem, as far as it is solved, is, as coming from Ibsen, very remarkable. It is not, as might have been expected after his long propaganda of Individualism, that they should break up the seraglio and go out into the world until they have learnt to stand alone, and through that to accept companionship on honorable conditions only. Ibsen here explicitly insists for the first time that "we are members one of another," and that though the strongest man is he who stands alone, the man who is standing alone for his own sake solely is literally an idiot. It is indeed a staring fact in history and contemporary life that nothing is so gregarious as selfishness, and nothing so solitary as the selflessness that loathes the word Altruism because to it there are no "others": it sees and feels in every man's case the image of its own. "Inasmuch as ye have done it unto one of the least of these my brethren ye have done it unto me" is not Altruism or Othersism. It is an explicit repudiation of the patronizing notion that "the least of these" is *another* to whom you are invited to be very nice and kind: in short, it accepts entire identification of "me" with "the least of these." The fashionably sentimental version, which runs, in effect, "If you subscribe eighteenpence to give this little dear a day in the country I shall regard it as a loan of one-and-sixpence to myself" is really more conceitedly remote from the spirit of the famous Christian saying than even the sham political economy that took in Mr. Gradgrind. Accordingly, if you would see industrial sweating at its vilest, you must go, not to the sempstresses who work for commercial firms, but to the victims of pious Altruistic Ladies' Work Guilds and the like, in which ladies with gold and green forests offer to "others" their blouses to be stitched at prices that the most sordid East End slave-driver would recoil from offering.

Thus we see that in Ibsen's mind, as in the actual history of the nineteenth century, the way to Communism lies through the most resolute and uncompromising Individualism. James Mill, with an inhuman conceit and pedantry which leaves the fable of Allmers and Eyolf far behind, educated John Stuart Mill to be the arch Individualist of his time, with the result that John Stuart Mill became a Socialist quarter of a century before the rest of his set moved in that direction. Herbert Spencer lived to write despairing pamphlets against the Socialism of his ablest pupils. There is no hope in Individualism for egotism. When a man is at last brought face to face with himself by a brave Individualism, he finds himself face to face, not with an individual, but with a species, and knows that to save himself, he must save the race. He can have no life except a share in the life of the community; and if that life is unhappy and squalid, nothing that he can do to paint and paper and upholster and shut off his little corner of it can really rescue him from it.

It happens so to that bold Individualist Mrs. Rita Allmers. The Allmers are, of course, snobs, and have always been very determined that the common little children down at the pier should be taught their place as Eyolf's inferiors. They even go the length of discussing whether these dirty little wretches should not be punished for their cowardice in not rescuing Eyolf. Thereby they raise the terrible question whether they themselves, who are afraid to commit suicide in their misery, would have been any braver. There is nobody to comfort them; for the income from the gold and green forests, by enabling them to cut themselves off from all industry of the place, has led them into something like total isolation. They hate their neighbors as themselves. They are alone together with nothing to do but wear each other out and drive each other mad to an extent impossible under any other conditions. And Rita's plight is the more desperate of the two, because as she has been the more unscrupulous, the more exacting, she has left him something to look forward to: freedom from her. He is bent on that, at least: he will not live with her on any terms, not stay anywhere within reach of her: the one thing he craves is that he may never see her or speak to her again. That is the end of the "two souls with but a single thought," &c. But to her his release is only a supreme privation, the end of everything that gave life any meaning for her. She has not even egotism to fall back on.

At this pass, an annoyance of which she has often complained occurs again. The children down at the pier make a noise, playing and yelling as if Eyolf had never existed. It suddenly occurs to her that these are children too, just like Eyolf, and that they are suffering a good deal from neglect. After all, they too are little Eyolfs. Inasmuch as she can do it unto one of the least of these his brethren she can do it unto him. She determines to take the dirty little wretches in hand and look after them. It is at all events a more respectable plan than that of the day before, which was to throw herself away on the first man she met if Allmers dared to think of anybody but her. And it has the domestic advantage that Allmers has nothing to fear from a woman who has something else to do than torment him with passions that devour and jealousies that enslave him. The world and the home suddenly take on their natural aspect. Allmers offers to stay and help her. And so they are delivered from their evil dream, and, let us hope, live happily ever after.

JOHN GABRIEL BORKMAN, 1896

In Little Eyolf the shadow of death lifted for a moment; but now we enter it again. Here the persons of the drama are not only dead but buried. Borkman is a Napoleon of finance. He has the root of finance in him in a born love of money in its final reality: a love, that is, of precious metals. He does not dream of beautiful ladies calling to him for knightly rescue from dragons and tyrants, but of metals imprisoned in undiscovered mines, calling to him to release them and send them out into all lands fertilizing, encouraging, creating. Music to him means the ring of the miner's pick and hammer: the eternal night underground is as magical to him as the moonlit starlit night of the upper air to the romantic poet. This love of metal is common enough: no man feels towards a cheque for £20 as he does towards twenty gold sovereigns: he will part from the paper with less of a pang than from the coins. There are misers whose fingers tremble when they touch gold, but close steadily on banknotes. True love of money is, in fact, a passion based on a physical appetite for precious metals. It is not greed: you cannot call a man who starves himself sooner than part with one sovereign from his sack of sovereigns, greedy. If he did the same for the love of God, you would call him a saint: if for the love of a woman, a perfect gentle knight. Men grow rich according to the strength of their obsession by this passion: its great libertines become Napoleons of finance: its narrow debauchees become misers, petty moneylenders, and the like. It must not be looked for in all our millionaires, because most of these are rich by pure accident (our abandonment of industry to the haphazard scrambles of private adventurers necessarily produces occasional windfalls which enrich the man who happens to be on the spot), as may be seen when the lucky ones are invited to display their supposed Napoleonic powers in spending their windfalls, when they reveal themselves as quite ordinary mortals, if not indeed sometimes as exceptionally resourceless ones. Besides, finance is one business, and industrial organization another: the man with a passion for altering the map by digging isthmuses never thinks of money save as a means to his end. But those who as financiers have passionately "made" money instead of merely holding their hats under an accidental shower of it will be found to have a genuine disinterested love of it. It is not easy to say how common this passion is. Poverty is general, which would seem to indicate a general lack of it; but poverty is mainly the result of organized robbery and oppression (politely called Capitalism) starving the passion for gold as it starves all the passions. The evidence is further confused by the decorative instinct: some men will load their fingers and shirtfronts with rings and studs, whilst others of equal means are ringless and fasten their shirts with sixpennorth of mother-of-pearl. But it is significant that Plato, and, following him, Sir Thomas More, saw with Ibsen, and made complete indifference to the precious metals, minted or not, a necessary qualification for aristocracy. This indifference is, as a matter of fact, so characteristic of our greatest non-industrial men that when they do not happen to inherit property they are generally poor and in difficulties. Therefore we who have never cared for money enough to do more than keep our heads above water, and are therefore tempted to regard ourselves as others regard us (that is, as failures, or, at best, as persons of no account) may console ourselves with the reflection that money-hunger is no more respectable than gluttony, and that unless its absence or feebleness is only a symptom of a general want of power to care for anything at all, it usually means that the soul has risen above it to higher concerns.

All this is necessary to the appreciation of Ibsen's presentment of the Napoleon of finance. Ibsen does not take him superficially: he goes to the poetic basis of the type: the love of gold—actual metallic gold—and the idealization of gold through that love.

Borkman meets the Misses Rentheim: two sisters: the elder richer than the younger. He falls in love with the younger; and she falls in love with him; but the love of gold is the master passion: he marries the elder. Yet he respects his secondary passion in the younger. When he speculates with other people's securities he spares hers. On the point of bringing off a great stroke of finance, the other securities are missed; and he is imprisoned for embezzlement. That is the end of him. He comes out of prison a ruined man and a dead man, and would not have even a tomb to sleep in but for the charity of Ella Rentheim, whose securities he spared when he broke her heart. She maintains his old home for him.

He now enters on the grimmest lying in state ever exposed to public view by mortal dramatist. His wife, a proud woman, must live in the same house with the convicted thief who has disgraced her, because she has nowhere else to lay her head; but she will not see him nor speak to him. She sits downstairs in the drawing-room eating the bitter bread of her sister's charity, and listening with loathing to her husband's steps as he paces to and fro in the long gallery upstairs "like a sick wolf." She listens not for days but for years. And her one hope is that her son Erhart will rehabilitate the family name; repay the embezzled money; and lead her from her tomb up again into honor and prosperity. To this task she has devoted *his* life.

Borkman has quite another plan. He is still Napoleon, and will return from his Elba to scatter his enemies and complete the stroke that ill-luck and the meddlesomeness of the law frustrated. But he is proud: prouder than Napoleon. He will not come back to the financial world until it finds out that it cannot do without him and comes to ask him to resume his place at the head of the board. He keeps himself in readiness for that deputation. He is always dressed for it; and when he hears steps on the threshold he stands up by the table; puts one hand into the breast of his coat; and assumes the attitude of a conqueror receiving suppliants. And this also goes on not for days but for years, long after the world has forgotten him, and there is nobody likely to come for him except Peer Gynt's button moulder.

Borkman, like all madmen, cannot nourish his delusion without some response from without. One of the victims of his downfall is a clerk who once wrote a tragedy, and has lived ever since in his own imagination as a poet. His family ridicules his tragedy and his pretensions; and as he is a poor ineffectual little creature who has never lived enough to feel dignified among the dead, like Borkman, he too finds it hard to keep his illusion alive without help. Fortunately he has admired Borkman, the great financier; and Borkman, when he has ruined him and ruined himself, is quite willing to be admired by this humble victim, and even to reward him by a pretence of believing in his poetic genius. Thus the two form one of those Mutual Admiration Societies on which the world so largely subsists, and make the years in the long gallery tolerable by flattering each other. There are even moments when Borkman is nerved to the point of starting for his second advent as a great financial redeemer. On such occasions the woman downstairs hears the footsteps of the sick wolf on the stairs approaching the hatstand where his hat and stick have waited unused all the years of his entombment; but they never reach that first stage of the journey. They always turn back into the gallery again.

This melancholy household of the dead crumbles to dust at the knock of the younger generation at the door. Erhart, dedicated by his mother to the task of paying his father's debts and retrieving his ruin, and by his aunt to the task of sweetening her last days with his grateful love, has dedicated himself to his own affairs—for the moment mostly love affairs—and has not the faintest intention of concerning himself with the bygone career of the crazy ex-felon upstairs or the sentimentalities of the old maid downstairs. He detests the house and the atmosphere, and associates his aunt's broken heart with nothing more important than the scent of stale lavender, which he dislikes. He spends his time happily in the house of a pretty lady in the neighborhood, who has been married and divorced, and knows how to form an adolescent youth. And as to the unpardonable enemy of the family, one Hinkel, who betrayed Borkman to the police and rose on his ruins, Erhart cares so little for that old story that he goes to Hinkel's parties and enjoys himself there very much. And when at last the pretty lady raises his standard of happiness to a point at which the old house and the old people become impossible, unthinkable, unbearable, he goes off with her to Italy and leaves the dead to bury their dead.

The details of this catastrophe make the play. The fresh air and the light of day break into the tomb; and its inhabitants crumble into dust. Foldal, the poet clerk, lets slip the fact that he has not the slightest belief in Borkman's triumphant return to the world; and Borkman retorts by telling him he is no poet. After this comedy comes the tragedy of the son's defection; and amid the recriminations of the broken heart, the baffled pride, and the shattered dreams, the castles in the air vanish and reveal the open grave they have hidden. Poor Foldal, limping home after being run over by a sledge in which his daughter is running away to act as "second string" and chaperone for Erhart and the pretty lady, is the only one who is wanted in the world, since he must still work for his derisive family. But Borkman returns to his dream, and ventures out of doors at last, not this time to resume his place as governor of the bank, but to release the imprisoned metal that rings and sings to him from the earth. In other words, to die in the open, mad but happy, whilst the two sisters, "we two shadows," end their strife over his body.

WHEN WE DEAD AWAKEN, 1900

This play, the last work of Ibsen, and at first the least esteemed, has had its prophecy so startlingly fulfilled in England that nobody will now question the intensity

of its inspiration. With us the dead have awakened in
the very manner prefigured in the play. The simplicity
and brevity of the story is so obvious, and the enormous
scope of the conception so difficult to comprehend,
that many of Ibsen's most devoted admirers failed to do
it justice. They knew that he was a man of seventy,
and were prepossessed with the belief that at such an
age his powers must be falling off. It certainly was
easier at that time to give the play up as a bad job than
to explain it. Now that the great awakening of women
which we call the Militant Suffrage Movement is upon
us, and you may hear our women publicly and passionately paraphrasing Ibsen's heroine without having read
a word of the play, the matter is simpler. There is no
falling-off here in Ibsen. It may be said that this is
physically impossible; but those who say so forget that
the natural decay of a writer's powers may shew itself
in two ways. The inferiority of the work produced is
only one way. The other is the production of equally
good or even better work with much greater effort
than it would have cost its author ten years earlier.
Ibsen produced this play with great difficulty in twice
as long a period as had before sufficed; and even at
that the struggle left his mind a wreck; for he not only
never wrote another play, but, like an overstrained
athlete, lost even the normal mental capacity of an
ordinary man. Yet it would be hard to say that the play
was not worth the sacrifice. It shews no decay of Ibsen's
highest qualities: his magic is nowhere more potent. It
is shorter than usual: that is all. The extraordinarily
elaborate private history, family and individual, of the
personages, which lies behind the action of the other
plays, is replaced by a much simpler history of a few
people in their general human relations without any
family history at all. And the characteristically conscientious fitting of the play to the mechanical conditions of old-fashioned stages has given way to demands
that even the best equipped and largest modern stages

cannot easily comply with; for the second act takes place in a valley; and though it is easy to represent a valley by a painted scene when the action is confined to one spot in the foreground, it is a different matter when the whole valley has to be practicable, and the movements of the figures cover distances which do not exist on the stage, and cannot, as far as my experience goes, be satisfactorily simulated by the stage carpenter, though they are easy enough for the painter. I should attach no importance at all to this in a writer less mindful of technical limitations and less ingenious in circumventing them than Ibsen, who was for some years a professional stage manager; but in his case it is clear that in calling on the theatre to expand to his requirements instead of, as his custom was, limiting his scene of action to the possibilities of a modest provincial theatre, he knew quite well what he was doing. Here then, we have three differences, from the earlier plays. None of them are inferiorities. They are proper to the difference of subject, and in fact increased the difficulty of the playwright's task by throwing him back on sheer dramatic power, unaided by the cheaper interest that can be gained on the stage by mere ingenuity of construction. Ibsen, who has always before played on the spectator by a most elaborate gradual development which would have satisfied Dumas, here throws all his cards on the table as rapidly as possible, and proceeds to deal intensively with a situation that never alters.

This situation is simple enough in its general statement, though it is so complex in its content that it raises the whole question of domestic civilization. Take a man and a woman at the highest pitch of natural ability and charm yet attained, and enjoying all the culture that modern art and literature can offer them; and what does it all come to? Contrast them with an essentially uncivilized pair, with a man who lives for hunting and eating and ravishing, and whose morals are those of the bully with the strong hand: in short, a man from the stone age as we conceive it (such men are still common enough in the classes that can afford the huntsman's life); and couple him with a woman who has no interest or ambition in life except to be captured by such a man (and of these we have certainly no lack). Then face this question. What is there to choose between these two pairs? Is the cultured gifted man less hardened, less selfish towards the women, than the paleolithic man? Is the woman less sacrificed, less enslaved, less dead spiritually in the one case than in the other? Modern culture, except when it has rotted into mere cynicism, shrieks that the question is an insult. The stone age, anticipating Ibsen's reply, guffaws heartily and says, "Bravo, Ibsen!" Ibsen's reply is that the sacrifice of the woman of the stone age to fruitful passions which she herself shares is as nothing compared to the wasting of the modern woman's soul to gratify the imagination and stimulate the genius of the modern artist, poet, and philosopher. He shews us that no degradation ever devized or permitted is as disastrous as this degradation; that through it women die into luxuries for men, and yet can kill them; that men and women are becoming conscious of this; and that what remains to be seen as perhaps the most interesting of all imminent social developments is what will happen "when we dead awaken."

Ibsen's greatest contemporary outside his own art was Rodin the French sculptor. Whether Ibsen knew this, or whether he was inspired to make his hero a sculptor just as Dickens was inspired to make Pecksniff an architect, is not known. At all events, having to take a type of the highest and ablest masculine genius, he made him a sculptor, and called his name, not Rodin, but Rubeck: a curious assonance, if it was not intentional. Rubeck is as able an individual as our civilization can produce. The difficulty of presenting such an individual in fiction is that it can be done only by a writer who occupies that position himself; for a dramatist cannot conceive anything higher than himself. No doubt he can invest an imaginary figure with all sorts of imaginary gifts. A drunken author may make his hero sober; an ugly, weak, puny, timid one may make him a Hyperion or a Hercules; a deaf mute may write novels in which the lover is an orator and his mistress a prima donna; but whatever ornaments and accomplishments he may pile up on his personages, he cannot give them greater souls than his own. Defoe could invent wilder adventures for Robinson Crusoe than Shakespear for Hamlet; but he could not make that mean adventurer, with his dull eulogies of the virtues of "the middle station of life," anything even remotely like Shakespear's prince.

For Ibsen this difficulty did not exist. He knew quite well that he was one of the greatest men living; so he simply said "Suppose ME to be a sculptor instead of a playwright," and the thing was done. Thus he came forward himself to plead to his own worst indictment of modern culture. One of the touches by which he identifies himself has all the irony of his earliest work. Rubeck has to make money out of human vanity, as all sculptors must nowadays, by portrait busts; but he revenges himself by studying and bringing out in his sitters "the respectable pompous horse faces, and self-opinionated donkey-muzzles, and lop-eared low-browed dog-skulls, and fatted swine-snouts, and dull brutal bull fronts" that lurk in so many human faces. All artists who deal with humanity do this, more or less. Leonardo da Vinci ruled his notebook in columns headed fox, wolf, etc., and made notes of faces by ticking them off in these columns, finding this, apparently, as satisfactory a memorandum as a drawing. Domestic animals, terriers, pugs, poultry, parrots, and cockatoos, are specially valuable to the caricaturist, as giving the original types which explain many faces. Ibsen must have classified his acquaintances a good deal in this way, not without an occasional chuckle; and his attribution of the practice to Rubeck is a confession of it.

Rubeck makes his reputation, as sculptors often do, by a statue of a woman. Not, be it observed, of a dress and a pair of boots, with a head protruding from them, but of a woman from the hand of Nature. It is worth noting here that we have hardly any portraits, either painted or carved, of our famous men and women or even of our nearest and dearest friends. Charles Dickens is known to us as a guy with a human head and face on top. Shakespear is a laundry advertisement of a huge starched collar with his head sticking out of it. Dr. Johnson is a face looking through a wig perched on a snuffy suit of old clothes. All the great women of history are fashion plates of their period. Bereaved parents, orphans, and widows weep fondly over photographs of uniforms, frock coats, gowns, and hats, for the sake of the little scrap of humanity that is allowed to peep through these trappings. Women with noble figures and plain or elderly faces are outdressed and outfaced by rivals who, if revealed as they really are, would be hardly human. Carlyle staggers humanity by inviting the House of Commons to sit unclothed, so that we, and they themselves, shall know them for what they really are.

Hence it is that the artist who adores mankind as his highest subject always comes back to the reality beneath the clothes. His claim to be allowed to do this is so irresistible that in every considerable city in England you will find, supported by the rates of prudish chapel goers, and even managed and inspected by committees of them, an art school where, in the "life class" (significant term!) young women posed in ridiculous and painful attitudes by a drawing master, and mostly under the ugliest circumstances of light, color, and surroundings, earn a laborious wage by allowing a crowd of art students to draw their undraped figures. It is a joylessly grotesque spectacle: one wonders whether anything can really be learnt from it; for never

have I seen one of these school models in an attitude
which any human being would, unless the alternative
were starvation, voluntarily sustain for thirty seconds,
or assume on any natural occasion or provocation whatever. Male models are somewhat less slavish; and the
stalwart laborer or olive-skinned young Italian who
poses before a crowd of easels with ludicrously earnest
young ladies in blue or vermilion gowns and em-
broidered pinafores drawing away at him for dear life
is usually much more comfortably and possibly posed.
But Life will not yield up her more intimate secrets for
eighteenpence an hour; and these earnest young ladies
and artsome young men, when they have filled port-
folios with such sordid life studies, know less about
living humanity than they did before, and very much
less about even the mechanism of the body and the
shape of its muscles than they could learn less in-
humanly from a series of modern kinematographs
of figures in motion.

Rubeck does not make his statues in a class at a
municipal art school by looking at a weary girl in a
tortured attitude with a background of match-board-
ing, under a roof of girders, and with the ghastly light
of a foggy, smoky manufacturing town making the
light side of her flesh dirty yellow and the shadowed
side putrid purple. He knows better than that. He finds
a beautiful woman, and tells her his vision of a statue
of The Resurrection Day in the form of a woman
"filled with a sacred joy at finding herself unchanged
in the higher, freer, happier region after the long
dreamless sleep of death." And the woman, immediately seizing his inspiration and sharing it, devotes herself to the work, not merely as his model, but as his
friend, his helper, fellow worker, comrade, all things,
save one, that may be humanly natural and necessary
between them for an unreserved co-operation in the
great work. The one exception is that they are not

lovers; for the sculptor's ideal is a virgin, or, as he calls it, a pure woman.

And her reward is that when the work is finished and the statue achieved, he says "Thank you for a priceless EPISODE," at which significant word, revealing as it does that she has, after all, been nothing to him but a means to his end, she leaves him and drops out of his life. To earn her living she must then pose, not to him, but before crowds in Variety Theatres in living pictures, gaining much money by her beauty, winning rich husbands, and driving them all to madness or to death by "a fine sharp dagger which she always has with her in bed," much as Rita Allmers nearly killed her husband. And she calls the statue her child and Rubeck's, as the book in Hedda Gabler was the child of Thea and Eilert Lövborg. But finally she too goes mad under the strain.

Rubeck presently meets a pretty Stone Age woman, and marries her. And as he is not a Stone Age man, and she is bored to distraction by his cultured interests, he disappoints her as thoroughly as she disgusts and wearies him: the symptoms being that though he builds her a splendid villa, full of works of art and so forth, neither he nor she can settle down quietly; and they take trips here, trips there, trips anywhere to escape being alone and at home together.

But the retribution for his egotism takes a much subtler form, and strikes at a much more vital place in him: namely, his artistic inspiration. Working with Irene, the lost model, he had achieved a perfect work of art; and, having achieved it, had supposed that he was done with her. But art is not so simple as that. The moment she forsakes him and leaves him to the Stone Age woman and to his egotism, he no longer sees the perfection of his work. He becomes dissatisfied with it. He sees that it can be improved: for instance, why should it consist of a figure of Irene alone? Why should he not be in it himself? Is he not a far more important factor in the conception? He changes the single figure design to a group. He adds a figure of himself. He finds that the woman's figure, with its wonderful expression of gladness, puts his own image out of countenance. He rearranges the group so as to give himself more prominence. Even so the gladness outshines him; and at last he "tones it down," striking the gladness out with his chisel, and making his own expression the main interest of the group. But he cannot stop there. Having destroyed the thing that was superior to him, he now wants to introduce things that are inferior. He carves clefts in the earth at the feet of his figure, and from these clefts he makes emerge the folk with the horse faces and the swine snouts that are nearer the beast than his own fine face. Then he is satisfied with his work; and it is in this form that it makes him famous and is finally placed in a public museum. In his days with Irene, they used to call these museums the prisons of works of art. Precisely what the Italian Futurist painters of today are calling them.

And now the play begins. Irene comes from her madhouse to a "health resort." Thither also comes Rubeck, wandering about with the Stone Age woman to avoid being left at home with her. Thither also comes the man of the Stone Age with his dogs and guns, and carries off the Stone Age woman, to her husband's great relief. Rubeck and Irene meet; and as they talk over old times, she learns, bit by bit, what has happened to the statue, and is about to kill him when she realizes, also bit by bit, that the history of its destruction is the history of his own, and that as he used her up and left her dead, so with her death the life went out of him. But, like Nora in A Doll's House, she sees the possibility of a miracle. The dead may awaken if only they can find an honest and natural relation in which they shall no longer sacrifice and slay one another. She asks him to climb to the top of a mountain with her and see that promised land. Half way up, they meet the Stone Age pair hunting. There is a storm coming. It is death to go up and danger to climb down. The Stone Age man faces the danger and carries his willing prey down. The others are beyond the fear of death, and go up. And that is the end of them and of the plays of Henrick Ibsen.

The end, too, let us hope, of the idols, domestic, moral, religious and political, in whose name we have been twaddled into misery and confusion and hypocrisy unspeakable. For Ibsen's dead hand still keeps the grip he laid on their masks when he first tore them off; and whilst that grip holds, all the King's horses and all the King's men will find it hard to set those Humpty-Dumpties up again.

THE LESSON OF THE PLAYS

IN FOLLOWING this sketch of the plays written by
Ibsen to illustrate his thesis that the real slavery of
today is slavery to ideals of goodness, it may be that
readers who have conned Ibsen through idealist specta-
cles have wondered that I could so pervert the utterances of a great poet. Indeed I know already that
many of those who are most fascinated by the poetry
of the plays will plead for any explanation of them
rather than that given by Ibsen himself in the plainest
terms through the mouths of Mrs. Alving, Relling,
and the rest. No great writer uses his skill to conceal
his meaning. There is a tale by a famous Scotch story-
teller which would have suited Ibsen exactly if he had
hit on it first. Jeanie Deans sacrificing her sister's life
on the scaffold to ideal truthfulness is far more horrible than the sacrifice in Rosmersholm; and the *deus
ex machina* expedient by which Scott makes the end of
his story agreeable is no solution of the ethical problem
raised, but only a puerile evasion of it. He dared not,
when it came to the point, allow Effie to be hanged
for the sake of Jeanie's ideals.[1] Nevertheless, if I were

[1] The common-sense solution of the ethical problem has often
been delivered by acclamation in the theatre. Many years ago
I witnessed a performance of a melodrama founded on this
story. After the painful trial scene, in which Jeanie Deans con-
demns her sister to death by refusing to swear to a perfectly
innocent fiction, came a scene in the prison. "If it had been me,"

to pretend that Scott wrote The Heart of Midlothian to shew that people are led to do as mischievous, as unnatural, as murderous things by their religious and moral ideals as by their envy and ambition, it would be easy to confute me from the pages of the book itself. And Ibsen, like Scott, has made his opinion plain. If any one attempts to maintain that Ghosts is a polemic in favor of indissoluble monogamic marriage, or that The Wild Duck was written to inculcate that truth should be told for its own sake, they must burn the text of the plays if their contention is to stand. The reason that Scott's story is tolerated by those who shrink from Ghosts is not that it is less terrible, but that Scott's views are familiar to all well-brought-up ladies and gentlemen, whereas Ibsen's are for the moment so strange to them as to be unthinkable. He is so great a poet that the idealist finds himself in the dilemma of being unable to conceive that such a genius should have an ignoble meaning, and yet equally unable to conceive his real meaning otherwise than as ignoble. Consequently he misses the meaning altogether in spite of Ibsen's explicit and circumstantial insistence on it, and proceeds to substitute a meaning congenial to his own ideal of nobility.

Ibsen's deep sympathy with his idealist figures seems to countenance this confusion. Since it is on the weaknesses of the higher types of character that idealism seizes, his most tragic examples of vanity, selfishness, folly, and failure are not vulgar villains, but men who in an ordinary novel or melodrama would be heroes. Brand and Rosmer, who drive those they love to death, do so with all the fine airs of the Sophoclean or Shakespearean good man persecuted by Destiny.

---

said the jailor, "I wad ha sworn a hole through an iron pot." The roar of applause which burst from the pit and gallery was thoroughly Ibsenist in sentiment. The speech, by the way, must have been a gag of the actor's: at all events I cannot find it in the acting edition of the play.

Hilda Wangel, who kills the Master Builder literally to amuse herself, is the most fascinating of sympathetic girl-heroines. The ordinary Philistine commits no such atrocities: he marries the woman he likes and lives with her more or less happily ever after; but that is not because he is greater than Brand or Rosmer: he is less. The idealist is a more dangerous animal that the Philistine just as a man is a more dangerous animal than a sheep. Though Brand virtually murdered his wife, I can understand many a woman, comfortably married to an amiable Philistine, reading the play and envying the victim her husband. For when Brand's wife, having made the sacrifice he has exacted, tells him that he was right; that she is happy now; that she sees God face to face; and then reminds him that "whoso sees Jehovah dies," he instinctively clasps his hands over her eyes; and that action raises him at once far above the criticism that sneers at idealism from beneath, instead of surveying it from the clear ether above, which can only be reached through its mists.

If, in my account of the plays, I have myself suggested false judgments by describing the errors of the idealists in the terms of the life they have risen above rather than in those of the life they fall short of, I can only plead, with but moderate disrespect for the general reader, that if I had done otherwise I should have failed wholly to make my exposition intelligible. Indeed accurate terms for realist morality, though they are to be found in the Bible, are so out of fashion and forgotten that in this very distinction between idealism and realism, I am forced to insist on a sense of the words which, had not Ibsen forced my hand, I should perhaps have conveyed otherwise, to avoid the conflict of many of its applications with the vernacular use of the words.

This, however, was a trifle compared to the difficulty which arose from our inveterate habit of labelling men with the abstract names of their qualities without the slightest reference to the underlying will which sets these qualities in action. At an anniversary celebration of the Paris Commune of 1871, I was struck by the fact that no speaker could find a eulogy for the Federals which would not have been equally appropriate to the peasants of La Vendée who fought for their tyrants against the French revolutionists, or to the Irishmen and Highlanders who fought for the Stuarts at the Boyne or Culloden. The statements that the slain members of the Commune were heroes who died for a noble ideal would have left a stranger quite as much in the dark about them as the counter statements, once common enough in our newspapers, that they were incendiaries and assassins. Our obituary notices are examples of the same ambiguity. Of all the public men lately deceased when Ibsenism was first discussed in England, none was made more interesting by strongly marked personal characteristics than the famous atheist orator Charles Bradlaugh. He was not in the least like any other notable member of the House of Commons. Yet when the obituary notices appeared, with the usual string of qualities: eloquence, determination, integrity, strong common-sense, and so on, it would have been possible, by merely expunging all names and other external details from these notices, to leave the reader entirely unable to say whether the subject of them was Gladstone, Lord Morley, William Stead, or any one else no more like Bradlaugh than Garibaldi or the late Cardinal Newman, whose obituary certificates of morality might nevertheless have been reprinted almost verbatim for the occasion without any gross incongruity. Bradlaugh had been the subject of many sorts of newspaper notices in his time. Thirty years ago, when the middle classes supposed him to be a revolutionist, the string of qualities which the press hung upon him were all evil ones, great stress being laid on the fact that as he was an atheist it would be an insult to God to admit him to Parliament. When it became apparent that he was an anti-socialist force in politics, he, without any recantation of his atheism, at once had the string of evil qualities exchanged for a rosary of good ones; but it is hardly necessary to add that neither the old badge nor the new could ever give any inquirer the least clue to the sort of man he actually was: he might have been Oliver Cromwell or Wat Tyler or Jack Cade, Penn or Wilberforce of Wellington, the late Mr. Hampden of flat-earth-theory notoriety or Proudhon or the Archbishop of Canterbury, for all the distinction such labels could give him one way or the other. The worthlessness of these abstract descriptions is recognized in practice every day. Tax a stranger before a crowd with being a thief, a coward, and a liar; and the crowd will suspend its judgment until you answer the question, "What's he done?" Attempt to take up a collection for him on the ground that he is an upright, fearless, high-principled hero; and the same question must be answered before a penny goes into the hat.

The reader must therefore discount those partialities which I have permitted myself to express in telling the stories of the plays. They are as much beside the mark as any other example of the sort of criticism which seeks to create an impression favorable or otherwise to Ibsen by simply pasting his characters all over with good or bad conduct marks. If any person cares to describe Hedda Gabler as a modern Lucretia who preferred death to dishonor, and Thea Elvsted as an abandoned, perjured strumpet who deserted the man she had sworn before her God to love, honor, and obey until her death, the play contains conclusive evidence establishing both points. If the critic goes on to argue that as Ibsen manifestly means to recommend Thea's conduct above Hedda's by making the end happier for her, the moral of the play is a vicious one, that, again, cannot be gainsaid. If, on the other hand, Ghosts be defended, as the dramatic critic of

Piccadilly did defend it, because it throws into divine
relief the beautiful figure of the simple and pious
Pastor Manders, the fatal compliment cannot be parried.
When you have called Mrs. Alving an emancipated woman or an unprincipled one, Alving a debau-
chee or a victim of society, Nora a fearless and noble-
hearted woman or a shocking little liar and an
unnatural mother, Helmer a selfish hound or a model
husband and father, according to your bias, you have
said something which is at once true and false, and
in both cases perfectly idle.

The statement that Ibsen's plays have an immoral
tendency, is, in the sense in which it is used, quite
true. Immorality does not necessarily imply mischievous conduct: it implies conduct, mischievous or not,
which does not conform to current ideals. All re-
ligions begin with a revolt against morality, and perish
when morality conquers them and stamps out such
words as grace and sin, substituting for them morality
and immorality. Bunyan places the town of Morality,
with its respectable leading citizens Mr. Legality and
Mr. Civility, close to the City of Destruction. In the
United States today he would be imprisoned for this.
Born as I was in the seventeenth century atmosphere
of mid-nineteenth century Ireland, I can remember
when men who talked about morality were suspected
of reading Tom Paine, if not of being downright
atheists. Ibsen's attack on morality is a symptom of
the revival of religion, not of its extinction. He is on
the side of the prophets in having devoted himself to
shewing that the spirit or will of Man is constantly
outgrowing the ideals, and that therefore thoughtless
conformity to them is constantly producing results
no less tragic than those which follow thoughtless
violation of them. Thus the main effect of his plays
is to keep before the public the importance of being
always prepared to act immorally. He reminds men
that they ought to be as careful how they yield to a

temptation to tell the truth as to a temptation to hold their tongues, and he urges upon women who either cannot or will not marry that the inducements held out to them by society to preserve their virginity and refrain from motherhood may be called temptations as logically as the inducements to the contrary held out by individuals and by their own temperaments, the practical decision depending on circumstances just as much as a decision between walking and taking a cab, however less trivial both the action and the circumstances may be. He protests against the ordinary assumption that there are certain moral institutions which justify all means used to maintain them, and insists that the supreme end shall be the inspired, eternal, ever growing one, not the external unchanging, artificial one; not the letter but the spirit; not the contract but the object of the contract; not the abstract law but the living will. And because the will to change our habits and thus defy morality arises before the intellect can reason out any racially beneficent purpose in the change, there is always an interval during which the individual can say no more than that he wants to behave immorally because he likes, and because he will feel constrained and unhappy if he acts otherwise. For this reason it is enormously important that we should "mind our own business" and let other people do as they like unless we can prove some damage beyond the shock to our feelings and prejudices. It is easy to put revolutionary cases in which it is so impossible to draw the line that they will always be decided in practice more or less by physical force; but for all ordinary purposes of government and social conduct the distinction is a commonsense one. The plain working truth is that it is not only good for people to be shocked occasionally, but absolutely necessary to the progress of society that they should be shocked pretty often. But it is not good for people to be garotted occasionally, or at all. That is why it is a mistake to treat an atheist as you treat a garotter, or to put "bad taste" on the footing of theft and murder. The need for freedom of evolution is the sole basis of toleration, the sole valid argument against Inquisitions and Censorships, the sole reason for not burning heretics and sending every eccentric person to the madhouse.

In short, our ideals, like the gods of old, are constantly demanding human sacrifices. Let none of them, says Ibsen, be placed above the obligation to prove itself worth the sacrifices it demands; and let everyone religiously refuse to sacrifice himself and others from the moment he loses his faith in the validity of the ideal. Of course it will be said here by incorrigibly slipshod readers that this, far from being immoral, is the highest morality; but I really will not waste further definition on those who will neither mean one thing or another by a word nor allow me to do so. Suffice it that among those who are not ridden by current ideals no question as to the ethical soundness of Ibsen's plays will ever arise; and among those who are so ridden his plays will be denounced as immoral, and cannot be defended against the accusation.

There can be no question as to the effect likely to be produced on an individual by his conversion from the ordinary acceptance of current ideals as safe standards of conduct, to the vigilant openmindedness of Ibsen. It must at once greatly deepen the sense of moral responsibility. Before conversion the individual anticipates nothing worse in the way of examination at the judgment bar of his conscience than such questions as, Have you kept the commandments? Have you obeyed the law? Have you attended church regularly? paid your rates and taxes to Cæsar? and contributed, in reason, to charitable institutions? It may be hard to do all these things; but it is still harder not to do them, as our ninety-nine moral cowards in the hundred well know. And even a scoundrel can do them all and

yet live a worse life than the smuggler or prostitute
who must answer No all through the catechism. Substitute for such a technical examination one in which
the whole point to be settled is, Guilty or Not Guilty?
one in which there is no more and no less respect for
virginity than for incontinence, for subordination than
for rebellion, for legality than for illegality, for piety
than for blasphemy: in short, for the standard qualities
than for the standard faults, and immediately, instead
of lowering the ethical standard by relaxing the tests of
worth, you raise it by increasing their stringency to
a point at which no mere Pharisaism or moral cowardice can pass them.

Naturally this does not please the Pharisee. The
respectable lady of the strictest Church principles,
who has brought up her children with such relentless
regard to their ideal morality that if they have any
spirit left in them by the time they arrive at years of
independence they use their liberty to rush deliriously
to the devil: this unimpeachable woman has always
felt it unjust that the respect she wins should be accompanied by deep-seated detestation, whilst the latest
spiritual heiress of Nell Gwynne, whom no respectable
person dare bow to in the street, is a popular idol. The
reason is—though the idealist lady does not know it—
that Nell Gwynne is a better woman than she; and the
abolition of the idealist test which brings her out a
worse one, and its replacement by the realist test which
would shew the true relation between them, would
be a most desirable step forward in public morals,
especially as it would act impartially, and set the good
side of the Pharisee above the bad side of the Bohemian
as ruthlessly as it would set the good side of the Bohemian above the bad side of the Pharisee.[2] For as

[2] The warning implied in this sentence is less needed now than
it was twenty years ago. The association of Bohemianism with
the artistic professions and with revolutionary political views
has been weakened by the revolt of the children of the Bo-

long as convention goes counter to reality in these matters, people will be led into Hedda Gabler's error of making an ideal of vice. If we maintain the convention that the distinction between Catherine of Russia and Queen Victoria, between Nell Gwynne and Mrs. Proudie, is the distinction between a bad woman and a good woman, we need not be surprised when those who sympathize with Catherine and Nell conclude that it is better to be a loose woman than a strict one, and go on recklessly to conceive a prejudice against teetotalism and monogamy, and a prepossession in favor of alcoholic excitement and promiscuous amours. Ibsen himself is kinder to the man who has gone his own way as a rake and a drunkard than to the man who is respectable because he dare not be otherwise. We find that the franker and healthier a boy is, the more certain is he to prefer pirates and highwaymen, or Dumas musketeers, to "pillars of society" as his favorite heroes of romance. We have already seen both Ibsenites and anti-Ibsenites who seem to think that the cases of Nora and Mrs. Elvsted are meant to establish a golden rule for women who wish to be "emancipated": the said golden rule being simply, Run away from your husband. But in Ibsen's view of life, that would come under the same condemnation as the ecclesiastical rule, Cleave to your husband until death do you part. Most people know of a case or two in which it would be wise for a wife to follow the example of Nora or even of Mrs. Elvsted. But they must also know cases in which the results of such a course would be as tragi-comic as those of Gregers Werle's attempt in The Wild Duck to do for the Ekdal household what Lona Hessel did for the Bernick household. What Ibsen insists on is that there is no golden

hemians against its domestic squalor and social outlawry. Bohemianism is now rather one of the stigmata of the highly conservative "smart sets" of the idle rich than of the studio, the stage, and the Socialist organizations. (1912.)

rule; that conduct must justify itself by its effect upon life and not by its conformity to any rule or ideal. And since life consists in the fulfilment of the will, which is constantly growing, and cannot be fulfilled today under the conditions which secured its fulfilment yesterday, he claims afresh the old Protestant right of private judgment in questions of conduct as against all institutions, the so-called Protestant Churches themselves included.

Here I must leave the matter, merely reminding those who may think that I have forgotten to reduce Ibsenism to a formula for them, that its quintessence is that there is no formula.

WHAT IS THE NEW ELEMENT
IN THE NORWEGIAN SCHOOL?

I now come to the question: Why, since neither human nature nor the specific talent of the playwright has changed since the days of Charles Dickens and Dumas *père*, are the works of Ibsen, of Strindberg, of Tolstoy, of Gorki, of Tchekov, of Brieux, so different from those of the great fictionists of the first half of the nineteenth century? Tolstoy actually imitated Dickens. Ibsen was not Dickens's superior as an observer, nor is Strindberg, nor Gorki, nor Tchekov, nor Brieux. Tolstoy and Ibsen together, gifted as they were, were not otherwise gifted or more gifted than Shakespear and Molière. Yet a generation which could read all Shakespear and Molière, Dickens and Dumas, from end to end without the smallest intellectual or ethical perturbation, was unable to get through a play by Ibsen or a novel by Tolstoy without having its intellectual and moral complacency upset, its religious faith shattered, and its notions of right and wrong conduct thrown into confusion and sometimes even reversed. It is as if these modern men had a spiritual force that was lacking in even the greatest of their forerunners. And yet, what evidence is there in the lives of Wagner, Ibsen, Tolstoy, Strindberg, Gorki, Tchekov, and Brieux, that they were or are better men in any sense than Shakespear, Molière, Dickens, and Dumas?

I myself have been told by people that the reading of a single book of mine or the witnessing of a single play has changed their whole lives; and among these are some who tell me that they cannot read Dickens at all, whilst all of them have read books and seen plays by authors obviously quite as gifted as I am, without finding anything more in them than pastime.

The explanation is to be found in what I believe to be a general law of the evolution of ideas. "Every jest is an earnest in the womb of time" says Peter Keegan in John Bull's Other Island. "There's many a true word spoken in jest" says the first villager you engage in philosophic discussion. All very serious revolutionary propositions begin as huge jokes. Otherwise they would be stamped out by the lynching of their first exponents. Even these exponents themselves have their revelations broken to them mysteriously through their sense of humor. Two friends of mine, travelling in remote parts of Spain, were asked by the shepherds what their religion was. "Our religion," replied one of them, a very highly cultivated author and traveller, with a sardonic turn, "is that there is no God." This reckless remark, taken seriously, might have provided nineteenth century scepticism with a martyr. As it was, the countryside rang with laughter for days afterwards as the stupendous joke was handed round. But it was just by tolerating the blasphemy as a joke that the shepherds began to build it into the fabric of their minds. Being now safely lodged there, it will in due time develop its earnestness; and at last travellers will come who will be taken quite seriously when they say that the imaginary hidalgo in the sky whom the shepherds call God does indeed not exist. And they will remain godless, and call their streets Avenue Paul Bert and so forth, until in due time another joker will arrive with sidesplitting intimations that Shakespear's "There's a divinity that shapes our ends, rough hew them how we will" was a strictly scientific statement of fact, and that "neo-Darwinism" consists for the most part of grossly unscientific statements of superstitious nonsense. Which jest will in its due time come to its own as very solid earnest.

The same phenomenon may be noticed in our attitude towards matters of fact so obvious that no dispute can arise as to their existence. And here the power of laughter is astonishing. It is not enough to say merely that men enable themselves to endure the unbearablest nuisances and the deadliest scourges by setting up a merry convention that they are amusing. We must go further and face the fact that they actually are amused by them—that they are not laughing with the wrong side of the mouth. If you doubt it, read the popular fiction of the pre-Dickensian age, from the novels of Smollett to Tom Cringle's Log. Poverty in rags is a joke, yellow fever is a joke, drunkenness is a joke, dysentery as a joke, kickings, floggings, falls, frights, humiliations, and painful accidents of all sorts are jokes. Henpecked husbands and termagant mothers-in-law are prime jokes. The infirmities of age and the inexperience and shyness of youth are jokes; and it is first-rate fun to insult and torment those that suffer from them.

We take some of these jokes seriously enough now. Humphrey Clinker may not have become absolutely unreadable (I have not tried him for more than forty years); but there is certainly a good deal in the book that is now simply disgusting to the class of reader that in its own day found it uproariously amusing. Much of Tom Cringle has become mere savagery: its humors are those of a donkey race. Also, the fun is forced: one sees beneath the determination of the old sea dog to put a hearty smiling English face on pain and discomfort, that he has not merely looked on at it, and that he did not really like it. The mask of laughter

wears slowly off the shames and the evils; but men
finally see them as they really are.

Sometimes the change occurs, not between two
generations, but actually in the course of a single work
by one author. Don Quixote and Mr. Pickwick are
recognized examples of characters introduced in pure
ridicule, and presently gaining the affection and finally
the respect of their authors. To them may be added
Shakespear's Falstaff. Falstaff is introduced as a subordi-
nate stage figure with no other function than to be
robbed by the Prince and Poins, who was originally
meant to be the *raisonneur* of the piece, and the chief
figure among the prince's dissolute associates. But
Poins soon fades into nothing, like several characters
in Dickens's early works; whilst Falstaff develops into
an enormous joke and an exquisitely mimicked human
type. Only in the end the joke withers. The question
comes to Shakespear: *Is* this really a laughing matter?
Of course there can be only one answer; and Shakespear gives it as best he can by the mouth of the prince
become king, who might, one thinks, have the decency
to wait until he has redeemed his own character before
assuming the right to lecture his boon companion.
Falstaff, rebuked and humiliated, dies miserably. His
followers are hanged, except Pistol, whose exclamation
"Old do I wax; and from my weary limbs honor is
cudgelled" is a melancholy exordium to an old age of
beggary and imposture.

But suppose Shakespear had begun where he left
off! Suppose he had been born at a time when, as the
result of a long propaganda of health and temperance,
sack had come to be called alcohol, alcohol had come
to be called poison, corpulence had come to be regarded as either a disease or a breach of good manners,
and a conviction had spread throughout society that
the practice of consuming "a half-pennyworth of
bread to an intolerable deal of sack" was the cause of
so much misery, crime, and racial degeneration that

whole States prohibited the sale of potable spirits altogether, and even moderate drinking was more and
more regarded as a regrettable weakness! Suppose (to
drive the change well home) the women in the great
theatrical centres had completely lost that amused indulgence for the drunken man which still exists in some
out-of-the-way places, and felt nothing but disgust
and anger at the conduct and habits of Falstaff and
Sir Toby Belch! Instead of Henry IV and The Merry
Wives of Windsor, we should have had something
like Zola's L'Assommoir. Indeed, we actually have
Cassio, the last of Shakespear's gentleman-drunkards,
talking like a temperance reformer, a fact which sug-
gests that Shakespear had been roundly lectured for
the offensive vulgarity of Sir Toby by some woman of
refinement who refused to see the smallest fun in
giving a knight such a name as Belch, with characteristics to correspond to it. Suppose, again, that the
first performance of The Taming of the Shrew had
led to a modern Feminist demonstration in the theatre,
and forced upon Shakespear's consideration a whole
century of agitatresses, from Mary Wollstonecraft to
Mrs. Fawcett and Mrs. Pankhurst, is it not likely that
the jest of Katharine and Petruchio would have become the earnest of Nora and Torvald Helmer?

In this light the difference between Dickens and
Strindberg becomes intelligible. Strindberg simply
refuses to regard the cases of Mrs. Raddle and Mrs.
Macstinger and Mrs. Jo Gargery as laughing matters.
He insists on taking them seriously as cases of a tyranny
which effects more degradation and causes more
misery than all the political and sectarian oppressions
known to history. Yet it cannot be said that Strindberg, even at his fiercest, is harder on women than
Dickens. No doubt his case against them is far more
complete, because he does not shirk the specifically
sexual factors in it. But this really softens it. If Dickens
had allowed us, were it but for an instant, to see Jo

Gargery and Mrs. Jo as husband and wife, he would perhaps have been accused by fools of immodesty; but we should have at least some more human impression than the one left by an unredeemed shrew married to a grown-up terrified child. It was George Gissing, a modern realist, who first pointed out the power and truth to nature of Dickens's women, and the fact that, funny as they are, they are mostly detestable. Even the amiable ones are silly and sometimes disastrous. When the few good ones are agreeable they are not specifically feminine: they are the Dickensian good man in petticoats; yet they lack that strength which they would have had if Dickens had seen clearly that there is no such species in creation as "Woman, lovely woman," the woman being simply the female of the human species, and that to have one conception of humanity for the woman and another for the man, or one law for the woman and another for the man, or one artistic convention for woman and another for man, or, for the matter of that, a skirt for the woman and a pair of breeches for the man, is as unnatural, and in the long run as unworkable, as one law for the mare and another for the horse. Roughly it may be said that all Dickens's studies from life of the differentiated creatures our artificial sex institutions have made of women are, for all their truth, either vile or ridiculous or both. Betsy Trotwood is a dear because she is an old bachelor in petticoats: a manly woman, like all good women: good men being equally all womanly men. Miss Havisham, an insanely womanly woman, is a horror, a monster, though a Chinese monster: that is, not a natural one, but one produced by deliberate perversion of her humanity. In comparison, Strindberg's women are positively amiable and attractive. The general impression that Strindberg's women are the revenge of a furious woman-hater for his domestic failures, whilst Dickens is a genial idealist (he had little better luck domestically, by the way), is produced

solely by Dickens either making fun of the affair or
believing that women are born so and must be admitted
to the fellowship of the Holy Ghost on a feminine
instead of a human basis; whilst Strindberg takes
womanliness with deadly seriousness as an evil not to
be submitted to for a moment without vehement
protest and demand for quite practicable reform. The
nurse in his play who wheedles her old nursling and
then slips a strait waistcoat on him revolts us; but she
is really ten times more lovable and sympathetic than
Sairey Gamp, an abominable creature whose very soul
is putrid, and who is yet true to life. It is very note-
worthy that none of the modern writers who take
life as seriously as Ibsen have ever been able to bring
themselves to depict depraved people so pitilessly as
Dickens and Thackeray and even the genial Dumas
père. Ibsen was grim enough in all conscience: no man
has said more terrible things both privately and publicly; and yet there is not one of Ibsen's characters
who is not, in the old phrase, the temple of the Holy
Ghost, and who does not move you at moments by the
sense of that mystery. The Dickens-Thackeray spirit
is, in comparison, that of a Punch and Judy showman,
who is never restrained from whacking his little figures
unmercifully by the sense that they, too, are images
of God, and, "but for the grace of God," very like
himself. Dickens does deepen very markedly towards
this as he grows older, though it is impossible to pretend that Mrs. Wilfer is treated with less levity than
Mrs. Nickleby; but to Ibsen, from beginning to end,
every human being is a sacrifice, whilst to Dickens he
is a farce. And there you have the whole difference.
No character drawn by Dickens is more ridiculous
than Hjalmar Ekdal in The Wild Duck, or more eccentric than old Ekdal, whose toy game-preserve in
the garret is more fantastic than the house of Miss
Havisham; and yet these Ekdals wring the heart whilst
Micawber and Chivery (who sits between the lines

of clothes hung out to dry because "it reminds him of groves" as Hjalmar's garret reminds old Ekdal of bear forests) only shake the sides.

It may be that if Dickens could read these lines he would say that the defect was not in him but in his readers; and that if we will return to his books now that Ibsen has opened our eyes we will have to admit that he also saw more in the soul of Micawber than mere laughing gas. And indeed one cannot forget the touches of kindliness and gallantry which ennoble his mirth. Still, between the man who occasionally remembered and the man who never forgot, between Dick Swiveller and Ulrik Brendel, there is a mighty difference. The most that can be said to minimize it is that some of the difference is certainly due to the difference in the attitude of the reader. When an author's works produce violent controversy, and are new, people are apt to read them with that sort of seriousness which is very appropriately called deadly: that is, with a sort of solemn paralysis of every sense except a quite abstract and baseless momentousness which has no more to do with the contents of the author's works than the horrors of a man in delirium tremens have to do with real rats and snakes. The Bible is a sealed literature to most of us because we cannot read it naturally and unsophisticatedly: we are like the old lady who was edified by the word Mesopotamia, or Samuel Butler's Chowbok, who was converted to Christianity by the effect on his imagination of the prayer for Queen Adelaide. Many years elapsed before those who were impressed with Beethoven's music ventured to enjoy it sufficiently to discover what a large part of it is a riot of whimsical fun. As to Ibsen, I remember a performance of The Wild Duck, at which the late Clement Scott pointed out triumphantly that the play was so absurd that even the champions of Ibsen could not help laughing at it. It had not occurred to him that Ibsen could laugh like other men. Not until an author has become so familiar that we are quite at our ease with him, and are up to his tricks of manner, do we cease to imagine that he is, relatively to older writers, terribly serious.

Still, the utmost allowance we can make for this difference does not persuade us that Dickens took the improvidence and futility of Micawber as Ibsen took the improvidence and futility of Hjalmar Ekdal. The difference is plain in the works of Dickens himself; for the Dickens of the second half of the nineteenth century (the Ibsen half) is a different man from the Dickens of the first half. From Hard Times and Little Dorrit to Our Mutual Friend every one of Dickens's books lays a heavy burden on our conscience without flattering us with any hopes of a happy ending. But from The Pickwick Papers to Bleak House you can read and laugh and cry and go happy to bed after forgetting yourself in a jolly book. I have pointed out elsewhere how Charles Lever, after producing a series of books in which the old manner of rollicking through life as if all its follies and failures were splendid jokes, and all its conventional enjoyments and attachments delightful and sincere, suddenly supplied the highly appreciative Dickens (as editor of All the Year Round) with a quite new sort of novel, called A Day's Ride: A Life's Romance, which affected both Dickens and the public very unpleasantly by the bitter but tonic flavor we now know as Ibsenism; for the hero began as that uproarious old joke, the boaster who, being a coward, is led into all sorts of dangerous situations, like Bob Acres and Mr. Winkle, and then unexpectedly made them laugh very much on the wrong side of their mouths, exactly as if he were a hero by Ibsen, Strindberg, Turgenieff, Tolstoy, Gorki, Tchekov, or Brieux. And here there was no question of the author being taken too gloomily. His readers, full of Charles O'Malley and Mickey Free, were approaching the work with the most unsuspicious confidence in its entire jollity. The shock to the security of their sense-less laughter caught them utterly unprepared; and they resented it accordingly.

Now that a reaction against realism has set in, and the old jolly ways are coming into fashion again, it is perhaps not so easy as it once was to conceive the extraordinary fascination of this mirthless comedy, this tragedy that stripped the soul naked instead of bedizening it in heroic trappings. But if you have not experienced this fascination yourself, and cannot conceive it, you may take my word for it that it exists, and operates with such power that it puts Shakespear himself out of countenance. And even for those who are in full reaction against it, it can hardly be possible to go back from the death of Hedwig Ekdal to the death of Little Nell otherwise than as a grown man goes down on all fours and pretends to be a bear for the amusement of his children. Nor need we regret this: there are noble compensations for our increase of wisdom and sorrow. After Hedwig you may not be able to cry over Little Nell, but at least you can read Little Dorrit without calling it twaddle, as some of its first critics did. The jests do not become poorer as they mature into earnest. It was not through joyless poverty of soul that Shelley never laughed, but through an enormous apprehension and realization of the gravity of things that seemed mere fun to other men. If there is no Swiveller and no Trabbs's boy in The Pilgrim's Progress, and if Mr. Badman is drawn as Ibsen would have drawn him and not as Sheridan would have seen him, it does not follow that there is less strength (and joy is a quality of strength) in Bunyan than in Sheridan and Dickens. After all, the salvation of the world depends on the men who will not take evil good-humoredly, and whose laughter destroys the fool instead of encouraging him. "Rightly to be great," said Shakespear when he had come to the end of mere buffoonery, "is greatly to find quarrel in a straw." The English cry of "Amuse us: take things easily: dress up the world prettily for us" seems mere cowardice to the strong souls that dare look facts in the face; and just so far as people cast off levity and idolatry they find themselves able to bear the company of Bunyan and Shelley, of Ibsen and Strindberg and the great Russian realists, and unable to tolerate the sort of laughter that African tribes cannot restrain when a man is flogged or an animal trapped and wounded. They are gaining strength and wisdom: gaining, in short, that sort of life which we call the life everlasting, a sense of which is worth, for pure well-being alone, all the brutish jollities of Tom Cringle and Humphrey Clinker, and even of Falstaff, Pecksniff, and Micawber.

THE TECHNICAL NOVELTY
IN IBSEN'S PLAYS

IT IS a striking and melancholy example of the preoccupation of critics with phrases and formulas to which they have given life by taking them into the tissue of their own living minds, and which therefore seem and feel vital and important to them whilst they are to everybody else the deadest and dreariest rubbish (this is the great secret of academic dryasdust), that to this day they remain blind to a new technical factor in the art of popular stage-play making which every considerable playwright has been thrusting under their noses night after night for a whole generation. This technical factor in the play is the discussion. Formerly you had in what was called a well made play an exposition in the first act, a situation in the second, and unravelling in the third. Now you have exposition, situation, and discussion; and the discussion is the test of the playwright. The critics protest in vain. They declare that discussions are not dramatic, and that art should not be didactic. Neither the playwrights nor the public take the smallest notice of them. The discussion conquered Europe in Ibsen's Doll's House; and now the serious playwright recognizes in the discussion not only the main test of his highest powers, but also the real centre of his play's interest. Sometimes

171

he even takes every possible step to assure the public beforehand that his play will be fitted with that newest improvement.

This was inevitable if the drama was ever again to be raised above the childish demand for fables without morals. Children have a settled arbitrary morality: therefore to them moralizing is nothing but an intolerable platitudinizing. The morality of the grown-up is also very largely a settled morality, either purely conventional and of no ethical significance, like the rule of the road or the rule that when you ask for a yard of ribbon the shopkeeper shall give you thirty-six inches and not interpret the word yard as he pleases, or else too obvious in its ethics to leave any room for discussion: for instance, that if the boots keeps you waiting too long for your shaving water you must not plunge your razor into his throat in your irritation, no matter how great an effort of self-control your forbearance may cost you.

Now when a play is only a story of how a villain tries to separate an honest young pair of betrothed lovers; to gain the hand of the woman by calumny; and to ruin the man by forgery, murder, false witness, and other commonplaces of the Newgate Calendar, the introduction of a discussion would clearly be ridiculous. There is nothing for sane people to discuss; and any attempt to Chadbandize on the wickedness of such crimes is at once resented as, in Milton's phrase, "moral babble."

But this sort of drama is soon exhausted by people who go often to the theatre. In twenty visits one can see every possible change rung on all the available plots and incidents out of which plays of this kind can be manufactured. The illusion of reality is soon lost: in fact it may be doubted whether any adult ever entertains it: it is only to very young children that the fairy queen is anything but an actress. But at the age when we cease to mistake the figures on the stage for *dramatis personae*, and know that they are actors and actresses, the charm of the performer begins to assert itself; and the child who would have been cruelly hurt by being told that the Fairy Queen was only Miss Smith dressed up to look like one, becomes the man who goes to the theatre expressly to see Miss Smith, and is fascinated by her skill or beauty to the point of delighting in plays which would be unendurable to him without her. Thus we get plays "written round" popular performers, and popular performers who give value to otherwise useless plays by investing them with their own attractiveness. But all these enterprises are, commercially speaking, desperately precarious. To begin with, the supply of performers whose attraction is so far independent of the play that their inclusion in the cast sometimes makes the difference between success and failure is too small to enable all our theatres, or even many of them, to depend on their actors rather than on their plays. And to finish with, no actor can make bricks entirely without straw. From Grimaldi to Sothern, Jefferson, and Henry Irving (not to mention living actors) we have had players succeeding once in a lifetime in grafting on to a play which would have perished without them some figure imagined wholly by themselves; but none of them has been able to repeat the feat, nor to save many of the plays in which he has appeared from failure. In the long run nothing can retain the interest of the playgoer after the theatre has lost its illusion for his childhood, and its glamor for his adolescence, but a constant supply of interesting plays; and this is specially true in London, where the expense and trouble of theatregoing have been raised to a point at which it is surprising that sensible people of middle age go to the theatre at all. As a matter of fact, they mostly stay at home.

Now an interesting play cannot in the nature of things mean anything but a play in which problems of conduct and character of personal importance to the audience are raised and suggestively discussed. People have a thrifty sense of taking away something from such plays: they not only have had something for their money, but they retain that something as a permanent possession. Consequently none of the commonplaces of the box office hold good of such plays. In vain does the experienced acting manager declare that people want to be amused and not preached at in the theatre; that they will not stand long speeches; that a play must not contain more than 18,000 words; that it must not begin before nine nor last beyond eleven; that there must be no politics and no religion in it; that breach of these golden rules will drive people to the variety theatres; that there must be a woman of bad character, played by a very attractive actress, in the piece; and so on and so forth. All these counsels are valid for plays in which there is nothing to discuss. They may be disregarded by the playwright who is a moralist and a debater as well as a dramatist. From him, within the inevitable limits set by the clock and by the physical endurance of the human frame, people will stand anything as soon as they are matured enough and cultivated enough to be susceptible to the appeal of his particular form of art. The difficulty at present is that mature and cultivated people do not go to the theatre, just as they do not read penny novelets; and when an attempt is made to cater for them they do not respond to it in time, partly because they have not the habit of playgoing, and partly because it takes too long for them to find out that the new theatre is not like all the other theatres. But when they do at last find their way there, the attraction is not the firing of blank cartridges at one another by actors, nor the pretence of falling down dead that ends the stage combat, nor the simulation of erotic thrills by a pair of stage lovers, nor any of the other tomfooleries called action, but the exhibition and discussion of the character and conduct of stage figures who are made to appear real by the art of the playwright and the performers.

This, then, is the extension of the old dramatic form effected by Ibsen. Up to a certain point in the last act, A Doll's House is a play that might be turned into a very ordinary French drama by the excision of a few lines, and the substitution of a sentimental happy ending for the famous last scene: indeed the very first thing the theatrical wiseacres did with it was to effect exactly this transformation, with the result that the play thus pithed had no success and attracted no notice worth mentioning. But at just that point in the last act, the heroine very unexpectedly (by the wiseacres) stops her emotional acting and says: "We must sit down and discuss all this that has been happening between us." And it was by this new technical feature: this addition of a new movement, as musicians would say, to the dramatic form, that A Doll's House conquered Europe and founded a new school of dramatic art.

Since that time the discussion has expanded far beyond the limits of the last ten minutes of an otherwise "well made" play. The disadvantage of putting the discussion at the end was not only that it came when the audience was fatigued, but that it was necessary to see the play over again, so as to follow the earlier acts in the light of the final discussion, before it became fully intelligible. The practical utility of this book is due to the fact that unless the spectator at an Ibsen play has read the pages referring to it beforehand, it is hardly possible for him to get its bearings at a first hearing if he approaches it, as most spectators still do, with conventional idealist prepossessions. Accordingly, we now have plays, including some of my own, which begin with discussion and end with action, and others in which the discussion interpenetrates the action from beginning to end. When Ibsen invaded England discussion had vanished from the stage; and women could not write plays. Within twenty years women were writing better plays than men; and these plays were passionate arguments from beginning to end. The action of such plays consists of a case to be argued. If the case is uninteresting or stale or badly conducted or obviously trumped up, the play is a bad one. If it is important and novel and convincing, or at least disturbing, the play is a good one. But anyhow the play in which there is no argument and no case no longer counts as serious drama. It may still please the child in us as Punch and Judy does; but nobody nowadays pretends to regard the well made play as anything more than a commercial product which is not in question when modern schools of serious drama are under discussion. Indeed within ten years of the production of A Doll's House in London, audiences had become so derisive of the more obvious and hack-neyed features of the methods of Sardou that it became dangerous to resort to them; and playwrights who persisted in "constructing" plays in the old French manner lost ground not for lack of ideas, but because their technique was unbearably out of fashion.

In the new plays, the drama arises through a conflict of unsettled ideals rather than through vulgar attachments, rapacities, generosities, resentments, ambitions, misunderstandings, oddities and so forth as to which no moral question is raised. The conflict is not between clear right and wrong: the villain is as conscientious as the hero, if not more so: in fact, the question which makes the play interesting (when it *is* interesting) is which is the villain and which the hero. Or, to put it an-other way, there are no villains and no heroes. This strikes the critics mainly as a departure from dramatic art; but it is really the inevitable return to nature which ends all the merely technical fashions. Now the natural is mainly the everyday; and its climaxes must be, if not everyday, at least everylife, if they are to have any im-portance for the spectator. Crimes, fights, big legacies, fires, shipwrecks, battles, and thunderbolts are mistakes in a play, even when they can be effectively simulated. No doubt they may acquire dramatic interest by putting a character through the test of an emergency; but the test is likely to be too obviously theatrical, because, as the playwright cannot in the nature of things have much experience of such catastrophes, he is forced to substitute a set of conventions or conjectures for the feelings they really produce.

In short, pure accidents are not dramatic: they are only anecdotic. They may be sensational, impressive, provocative, ruinous, curious, or a dozen other things; but they have no specifically dramatic interest. There is no drama in being knocked down or run over. The catastrophe in Hamlet would not be in the least dramatic had Polonius fallen downstairs and broken his neck, Claudius succumbed to delirium tremens, Hamlet forgotten to breathe in the intensity of his philosophic speculation, Ophelia died of Danish measles, Laertes been shot by the palace sentry, and Rosencrantz and Guildenstern drowned in the North Sea. Even as it is, the Queen, who poisons herself by accident, has an air of being polished off to get her out of the way: her death is the one dramatic failure of the piece. Bushels of good paper have been inked in vain by writers who imagined they could produce a tragedy by killing everyone in the last act accidentally. As a matter of fact no accident, however sanguinary, can produce a moment of real drama, though a difference of opinion between husband and wife as to living in town or country might be the beginning of an appalling tragedy or a capital comedy.

It may be said that everything is an accident: that Othello's character is an accident, Iago's character another accident, and the fact that they happened to come together in the Venetian service an even more accidental accident. Also that Torvald Helmer might just as likely have married Mrs. Nickleby as Nora. Granting this trifling for what it is worth, the fact remains that marriage is no more an accident than birth or death: that is, it is expected to happen to everybody. And if every man has a good deal of Torvald Helmer in him, and every woman a good deal of Nora, neither their characters nor their meeting and marrying are accidents. Othello, though entertaining, pitiful, and resonant with the thrills a master of language can produce by mere artistic sonority is certainly much more accidental than A Doll's House; but it is correspondingly less important and interesting to us. It has been kept alive, not by its manufactured misunderstandings and stolen handkerchiefs and the like, nor even by its orchestral verse, but by its exhibition and discussion of human nature, marriage, and jealousy; and it would be a prodigiously better play if it were a serious discussion of the highly interesting problem of how a simple Moorish soldier would get on with a "supersubtle" Venetian lady of fashion if he married her. As it is, the play turns on a mistake; and though a mistake can produce a murder, which is the vulgar substitute for a tragedy, it cannot produce a real tragedy in the modern sense. Reflective people are not more interested in the Chamber of Horrors than in their own homes, nor in murderers, victims, and villains than in themselves; and the moment a man has acquired sufficient reflective power to cease gaping at waxworks, he is on his way to losing interest in Othello, Desdemona, and Iago exactly to the extent to which they become interesting to the police. Cassio's weakness for drink comes much nearer home to most of us than Othello's strangling and throat cutting, or Iago's theatrical confidence trick. The proof is that Shakespear's professional colleagues, who exploited all his sensational devices, and piled up torture on murder and incest on adultery until they had far out-Heroded Herod, are now unmemorable and unplayable. Shakespear survives because he coolly treated the sensational horrors of his borrowed plots as inorganic theatrical accessories, using them simply as pretexts for dramatizing human character as it exists in the normal world. In enjoying and discussing his plays we unconsciously discount the combats and murders: commentators are never so astray (and consequently so ingenious) as when they take Hamlet seriously as a madman, Macbeth as a homicidal Highlander, and impish humorists like Richard and Iago as lurid villains of the Renascence. The plays in which these figures appear could be changed into comedies without altering a hair of their beards. Shakespear, had anyone been intelligent enough to tax him with this, would perhaps have said that most crimes are accidents that happen to people exactly like ourselves, and that Macbeth, under propitious circumstances, would have made an exemplary rector of Stratford, a real criminal being a defective monster, a human accident, useful on the stage only for minor parts such as Don Johns, second murderers, and the like. Anyhow, the fact remains that Shakespear survives by what he has in common with Ibsen, and not by what he has in common with Webster and the rest. Hamlet's surprise at finding that he "lacks gall" to behave in the idealistically conventional manner, and that no extremity of rhetoric about the duty of revenging "a dear father slain" and exterminating the "bloody bawdy villain" who murdered him seems to make any difference in their domestic relations in the palace in Elsinore, still keeps us talking about him and going to the theatre to listen to him, whilst the older Hamlets, who never had any Ibsenist hesitations, and shammed madness, and entangled the courtiers in the arras and burnt them, and stuck hard to the theatrical school of the fat boy in Pickwick ("I wants to make your flesh creep"), are as dead as John Shakespear's mutton.

We have progressed so rapidly on this point under the impulse given to the drama by Ibsen that it seems strange now to contrast him favorably with Shakespear on the ground that he avoided the old catastrophes which left the stage strewn with the dead at the end of an Elizabethan tragedy. For perhaps the most plausible reproach levelled at Ibsen by modern critics of his own school is just that survival of the old school in him which makes the death rate so high in his last acts. Do Oswald Alving, Hedvig Ekdal, Rosmer and Rebecca, Hedda Gabler, Solness, Eyolf, Borkman, Rubeck and Irene die dramatically natural deaths, or are they slaughtered in the classic and Shakespearean manner, partly because the audience expects blood for its money, partly because it is difficult to make people attend seriously to anything except by startling them with some violent calamity? It is so easy to make out a case for either view that I shall not argue the point. The post-Ibsen playwrights apparently think that Ibsen's homicides and suicides were forced. In Tchekov's Cherry Orchard, for example, where the sentimental ideals of our amiable, cultured, Schumann playing propertied class are reduced to dust and ashes by a hand not less deadly than Ibsen's because it is so much more caressing, nothing more violent happens than that the family cannot afford to keep up its old house. In Granville-Barker's plays, the campaign against our society is carried on with all Ibsen's implacability; but the one suicide (in Waste) is unhistorical; for neither Parnell nor Dilke, who were the actual cases in point of the waste which was the subject of the play, killed himself. I myself have been reproached because the characters in my plays "talk but do nothing," meaning that they do not commit felonies. As a matter of fact we have come to see that it is no true *dénouement* to cut the Gordian knot as Alexander did with a stroke of the sword. If people's souls are tied up by law and public opinion it is much more tragic to leave them to wither in these bonds than to end their misery and relieve the salutary compunction of the audience by outbreaks of violence. Judge Brack was, on the whole, right when he said that people dont do such things. If they did, the idealists would be brought to their senses very quickly indeed.

But in Ibsen's plays the catastrophe, even when it seems forced, and when the ending of the play would be more tragic without it, is never an accident; and the play never exists for its sake. His nearest to an accident is the death of little Eyolf, who falls off a pier and is drowned. But this instance only reminds us that there is one good dramatic use for an accident: it can awaken people. When England wept over the deaths of little Nell and Paul Dombey, the strong soul of Ruskin was moved to scorn: to novelists who were at a loss to make their books sell he offered the formula: When at a loss, kill a child. But Ibsen did not kill little Eyolf to manufacture pathos. The surest way to achieve a thoroughly bad performance of Little Eyolf is to conceive it as a sentimental tale of a drowned darling. Its drama lies in the awakening of Allmers and his wife to the despicable quality and detestable rancors of the life they have been idealizing as blissful and poetic. They are so sunk in their dream that the awakening can be effected only by a violent shock. And that is just the one dramatically useful thing an accident can do. It can shock. Hence the accident that befalls Eyolf.

As to the deaths in Ibsen's last acts, they are a sweeping up of the remains of dramatically finished people. Solness's fall from the tower is as obviously symbolic as Phaeton's fall from the chariot of the sun. Ibsen's dead bodies are those of the exhausted or destroyed: he does not kill Hilda, for instance, as Shakespear killed Juliet. He is ruthless enough with Hedvig and Eyolf because he wants to use their deaths to expose their parents; but if he had written Hamlet nobody would have been killed in the last act except perhaps Horatio, whose correct nullity might have provoked Fortinbras to let some of the moral sawdust out of him with his sword.

For Shakespearean deaths in Ibsen you must go back to Lady Inger and the plays of his nonage, with which this book is not concerned.

The drama was born of old from the union of two desires: the desire to have a dance and the desire to hear a story. The dance became a rant: the story became a situation. When Ibsen began to make plays, the art of the dramatist had shrunk into the art of contriving a situation. And it was held that the stranger the situation, the better the play. Ibsen saw that, on the contrary, the more familiar the situation, the more interesting the play. Shakespear had put ourselves on the stage but not our situations. Our uncles seldom murder our fathers, and cannot legally marry our mothers; we do not meet witches; our kings are not as a rule stabbed and succeeded by their stabbers; and when we raise money by bills we do not promise to pay pounds of our flesh. Ibsen supplies the want left by Shakespear. He gives us not only ourselves, but ourselves in our own situations. The things that happen to his stage figures are things that happen to us. One consequence is that his plays are much more important to us than Shakespear's. Another is that they are capable both of hurting us cruelly and of filling us with excited hopes of escape from idealistic tyrannies, and with visions of intenser life in the future.

Changes in technique follow inevitably from these changes in the subject matter of the play. When a dramatic poet can give you hopes and visions, such old maxims as that stage-craft is the art of preparation become boyish, and may be left to those unfortunate playwrights who, being unable to make anything really interesting happen on the stage, have to acquire the art of continually persuading the audience that it is going to happen presently. When he can stab people to the heart by shewing them the meanness or cruelty of something they did yesterday and intend to do tomorrow, all the old tricks to catch and hold their attention

become the silliest of superfluities. The play called The
Murder of Gonzago, which Hamlet makes the players
act before his uncle, is artlessly constructed; but it
produces a greater effect on Claudius than the Œdipus
of Sophocles, because it is about himself. The writer
who practises the art of Ibsen therefore discards all the
old tricks of preparation, catastrophe, *dénouement,* and
so forth without thinking about it, just as a modern
rifleman never dreams of providing himself with powder horns, percussion caps, and wads: indeed he does
not know the use of them. Ibsen substituted a terrible
art of sharpshooting at the audience, trapping them,
fencing with them, aiming always at the sorest spot in
their consciences. Never mislead an audience, was an
old rule. But the new school will trick the spectator
into forming a meanly false judgment, and then convict
him of it in the next act, often to his grievous mortifica-
tion. When you despise something you ought to take
off your hat to, or admire and imitate something you
ought to loathe, you cannot resist the dramatist who
knows how to touch these morbid spots in you and
make you see that they are morbid. The dramatist
knows that as long as he is teaching and saving his
audience, he is as sure of their strained attention as a
dentist is, or the Angel of the Annunciation. And
though he may use all the magic of art to make you
forget the pain he causes you or to enhance the joy of
the hope and courage he awakens, he is never occupied
in the old work of manufacturing interest and expecta-
tion with materials that have neither novelty, significance, nor relevance to the experience or prospects of
the spectators.

Hence a cry has arisen that the post-Ibsen play is not
a play, and that its technique, not being the technique
described by Aristotle, is not a technique at all. I will
not enlarge on this: the fun poked at my friend Mr.
A. B. Walkley in the prologue of Fanny's First Play
need not be repeated here. But I may remind him that

the new technique is new only on the modern stage. It has been used by preachers and orators ever since speech was invented. It is the technique of playing upon the human conscience; and it has been practised by the playwright whenever the playwright has been capable of it. Rhetoric, irony, argument, paradox, epigram, parable, the rearrangement of haphazard facts into orderly and intelligent situations: these are both the oldest and the newest arts of the drama; and your plot construction and art of preparation are only the tricks of theatrical talent and the shifts of moral sterility, not the weapons of dramatic genius. In the theatre of Ibsen we are not flattered spectators killing an idle hour with an ingenious and amusing entertainment: we are "guilty creatures sitting at a play"; and the technique of pastime is no more applicable than at a murder trial.

The technical novelties of the Ibsen and post-Ibsen plays are, then: first, the introduction of the discussion and its development until it so overspreads and interpenetrates the action that it finally assimilates it, making play and discussion practically identical; and, second, as a consequence of making the spectators themselves the persons of the drama, and the incidents of their own lives its incidents, the disuse of the old stage tricks by which audiences had to be induced to take an interest in unreal people and improbable circumstances, and the substitution of a forensic technique of recrimination, disillusion, and penetration through ideals to the truth, with a free use of all the rhetorical and lyrical arts of the orator, the preacher, the pleader, and the rhapsodist.

NEEDED: AN IBSEN THEATRE

It MUST now be plain to my readers that the doctrine taught by Ibsen can never be driven home from the stage whilst his plays are presented to us in haphazard order at the commercial theatres. Indeed our commercial theatres are so well aware of this that they have from the first regarded Ibsen as hopelessly uncommercial: he might as well never have lived as far as they are concerned. Even the new advanced theatres which now deal freely with what I have called post-Ibsenist plays hardly meddle with him. Had it not been for the great national service disinterestedly rendered by Mr. William Archer in giving us a complete translation of Ibsen's plays (a virtually unremunerated public service which I hope the State will recognize fitly), Ibsen would be less known in England than Swedenborg. By losing his vital contribution to modern thought we are losing ground relatively to the countries which, like Germany, have made his works familiar to their play-goers. But even in Germany Ibsen's meaning is seen only by glimpses. What we need is a theatre devoted primarily to Ibsen as the Bayreuth Festspielhaus is devoted to Wagner. I have shewn how the plays, as they succeed one another, are parts of a continuous discussion; how the difficulty left by one is dealt with in the next; how Mrs. Alving is a reply to your hasty remark that Nora Helmer ought to be ashamed of herself for leaving her husband; how Gregers Werle warns you not to be as great a fool in your admiration of Lona Hessel as of Patient Grisel. The plays should, like Wagner's Ring, be performed in cycles; so that Ibsen may hunt you down from position to position until you are finally cornered.

The larger truth of the matter is that modern European literature and music now form a Bible far surpassing in importance to us the ancient Hebrew Bible that has served us so long. The notion that inspiration is something that happened thousands of years ago, and was then finished and done with, never to occur again: in other words, the theory that God retired from business at that period and has not since been heard from, is as silly as it is blasphemous. He who does not believe that revelation is continuous does not believe in revelation at all, however familiar his parrot's tongue and pewsleepy ear may be with the word. There comes a time when the formula "Also sprach Zarathustra" succeeds to the formula "Thus saith the Lord," and when the parable of the doll's house is more to our purpose than the parable of the prodigal son. When Bunyan published The Pilgrim's Progress, his first difficulty was with the literal people who said, "There is no such individual in the directory as Christian, and no such place in the gazetteer as the City of Destruction: therefore you are a liar." Bunyan replied by citing the parables: asking, in effect, whether the story of the wise and foolish virgins is also a lie. A couple of centuries or so later, when I myself wrote a play for the Salvation Army to shew them that the dramatic method might be used for their gospel as effectively as the lyric or orchestral method, I was told that unless I could guarantee that the persons in my play actually existed, and the incidents had actually occurred, I, like Bunyan, would be regarded by the elderly soldiers in the army as no better than Ananias. As it was useless for me to try to make these simple souls understand that in real life truth is revealed by parables and false-hood supported by facts, I had to leave the army to its oratorical metaphors and to its popular songs about heartbroken women waiting for the footsteps of their drunken husbands, and hearing instead the joyous step of the converted man whose newly found salvation will dry all their tears. I had not the heart to suggest that these happy pairs were as little authentic as The Second Mrs. Tanqueray; for I spied behind the army's con-fusion of truth with mere fact the old doubt whether anything good can come out of the theatre, a doubt as inveterate and neither more nor less justifiable than the doubt of our Secularists whether anything good can come out of the gospels.

But I think Ibsen has proved the right of the drama to take scriptural rank, and his own right to canonical rank as one of the major prophets of the modern Bible. The sooner we recognize that rank and give up the idea of trying to make a fashionable entertainment of his plays the better. It ends in our not performing them at all, and remaining in barbarous and dangerous igno-rance of the case against idealism. We want a frankly doctrinal theatre. There is no more reason for making a doctrinal theatre inartistic than for putting a cathedral organ out of tune: indeed all experience shews that doctrine alone nerves us to the effort called for by the greatest art. I therefore suggest that even the sciolists and voluptuaries who care for nothing in art but its luxuries and its executive feats are as strongly interesced in the establishment of such a theatre as those for whom the What is always more important than the How, if only because the How cannot become really magical until such magic is indispensable to the revelation of an all-important What.

I do not suggest that the Ibsen theatre should confine itself to Ibsen any more than the Established Church confines itself to Jeremiah. The post-Ibsenists could also be expounded there; and Strindberg should have his place, were it only as Devil's Advocate. But performances should be in the order of academic courses, designed so as to take audiences over the whole ground as Ibsen and his successors took them; so that the exposition may be consecutive. Otherwise the doctrine will not be interesting, and the audiences will not come regularly. The efforts now being made to regenerate the drama are often wasted through lack of doctrinal conviction and consequent want of system, the net result being an irresolute halting between the doctrinal and the merely entertaining.

For this sort of enterprise an endowment is necessary, because commercial capital is not content in a theatre with reasonable interest: it demands great gains even at the cost of great hazards. Besides, nobody will endow mere pleasure, whereas doctrine can always command endowment. It is the foolish disclaiming of doctrine that keeps dramatic art unendowed. When we ask for an endowed theatre we always take the greatest pains to assure everybody that we do not mean anything unpleasantly serious, and that our endowed theatre will be as bright and cheery (meaning as low and common) as the commercial theatres. As a result of which we get no endowment. When we have the sense to profit by this lesson and promise that our endowed theatre will be an important place, and it will make people of low tastes and tribal or commercial ideas horribly uncomfortable by its efforts to bring conviction of sin to them, we shall get endowment as easily as the religious people who are not foolishly ashamed to ask for what they want.

DRAMABOOKS

WHEN ORDERING, please use the Standard Book Number consisting of the publisher's prefix, 8090–, plus the five digits following each title. (Note that the numbers given in this list are for paperback editions only. Many of the books are also available in cloth.)

For a complete list of plays (including the New Mermaids and Spotlight Dramabooks series), please write to Hill and Wang, 72 Fifth Avenue, New York, New York 10011.